OVER

P. J. CLARKE'S BAR

OVER

P. J. CLARKE'S BAR

TALES FROM

NEW YORK CITY'S FAMOUS SALOON

HELEN MARIE CLARKE

Skyhorse Publishing

Skyhorse Publishing books may be purchased in bulk at special discounts for sales promotion, corporate gifts, fund-raising, or educational purposes. Special editions can also be created to specifications. For details, contact the Special Sales Department, Skyhorse Publishing, 307 West 36th Street, 11th Floor, New York, NY 10018 info@skyhorsepublishing.com.

www.skyhorsepublishing.com
10 9 8 7 6 5 4 3 2 1

Library of Congress Cataloging-in-Publication Data

Clarke, Helen Marie.
Over P. J. Clarke's Bar: Tales from New York City's Famous Saloon/Helen Marie Clarke.
pages cm
ISBN 978-1-62087-197-3 (hard cover: alk. paper)
1. P. J. Clarke's Bar (New York, N.Y.)—History.   2. Irish Americans—New York (State)—New York—Social life and customs.   3. New York (N.Y.)—Social life and customs—20th century.   4. Bars (Drinking establishments)—New York (State)—New York—History. I. Title.
TX950.57.N7C53 2012
647.95747—dc23

2012025442

Printed in the United States of America

Over P. J.'s is dedicated to the Clarke family, especially to my parents, Helen and John Clarke, who were elegant and generous, and led their lives with integrity. Years ago they were the first to hear how much I wanted to tell the tale of P. J. Clarke's and the family who lived over the saloon. My husband, John Molanphy, and our three sons, Paul, Brian, and Tom, gave me the kind of support I needed to write this book.

Many thanks go to my first editor, Vanessa Fox O'Loughlin, for her patience and intelligence. Vanessa is located in Dublin and can be reached at www.ie.writing.com. I am also grateful for the excellent editing and guidance from senior editor Jennifer McCartney at Skyhorse Publishing.

COMPLIMENTS OF -

P. J. CLARKE

915 THIRD AVENUE

TELEPHONE. 1609 PLAZA

Miles' Cream Ale shall never fail to quench a thirsty throttle,

The imported wines are very fine to make the weary frisky,

But there is nothing made that can compare or equal Clarke's whiskey,

As they all say Clarke's for good whiskey it is a household expression and a family suggestion

To beat Clarke's whiskey is out of the question

With a Patrick Henry Cigar.

Contents

Introduction

WHAT IS IT ABOUT P. J. CLARKE'S MANHATTAN SALOON THAT HAS attracted the likes of Frank Sinatra, Marilyn Monroe, Jacqueline Kennedy, Nat King Cole, Rocky Graziano, Johnny Carson, Woody Allen, and Buddy Holly? There are few bars that match the clientele at Clarke's for both diversity and fame—working-class folks, entertainers, athletes, business executives, and members of New York society—all enjoying an escape from modern life in an Irish bar located in one of the oldest Victorian buildings still in use, next to a forty-seven-story high-rise on 3rd Avenue and East 55th Street. In a city known for tearing down its old buildings, P. J. Clarke's is special.

Celebrities who frequent P. J. Clarke's include athletes such as Wayne Gretsky and Barry Switzer, as well as entertainers such

Welcome to P. J. Clarke's – 2012

as Sigourney Weaver, Ben Kingsley, Tony Bennett, Sharon Stone, Peter O'Toole, and Michael Flatley of Riverdance fame. Despite having diverse careers, these athletes, musicians, and actors have one thing in common—they love P. J. Clarke's. I too have had a love affair with the saloon founded by my granduncle, Patrick Joseph Clarke, (aka "Paddy") 100 years ago, in 1912, and now owned by Clarke's Group.

The Irish call their pubs a "third place." The pub is neither a home, the first place, nor work, place number two—it is a third place, a neutral ground. The pub erases the distinction between a host and a guest, unlike a private party or gathering. For the Irish, conversation in the pub is the primary activity, along with drinking; the best pub is family owned and operated and is unpretentious with modest decor. And, best of all, the Irish pub lets people be playful and feel at home.

P. J. Clarke's playfulness was what made my granduncle's saloon the best third place for me, a location where I can never remember being unhappy—and it had nothing to do with the alcohol. Rather, it is the history and the charm of Clarke's that so many people (myself included) have enjoyed. And the food is reasonable and good and the conversation lively. Perhaps the celebrities who flock to P. J. Clarke's are especially in need of a third place because they often live in a fish bowl—they too like its playful atmosphere and, in turn, we ordinary folks enjoy rubbing elbows with them.

P. J. Clarke's was founded by an Irishman almost "straight off the boat." On the day in 1912 when my granduncle took possession of the saloon, which had been serving alcohol since 1884, he had a sign-maker paint gold letters spelling CLARKE'S on the window. Above the saloon were several flats—one of them rented by Paddy himself, which he later shared with my grandparents, James and Mary Clarke, and their six sons, the eldest of whom was my father, John. The Clarke family lived over the saloon from 1916 until 1937—hence the title for this memoir.

Paddy Clarke's neighborhood saloon survived Prohibition and evolved into one of the most popular watering holes in New York City. After Paddy died in 1948, his nephew, Charlie Clarke, stayed on as manager under the new owners, the Lavezzo family; it was under their leadership that the saloon became known as the "little bar that could." Beyond withstanding the Prohibition years, the saloon survived East Side Manhattan development in the 1960s, and bankruptcy in the 1990s—and today it is an Upper East Side historical landmark.

In 1945, when a glass of beer cost $.15 and a shot of whiskey $.35, Hollywood director Billy Wilder used P. J. Clarke's mahogany bar as a setting for his film, *The Lost Weekend*, a story about an alcoholic writer. My granduncle would have been surprised that *The Lost Weekend* was not the only film to use his bar as a locale. The main character in *French Connection II*, Popeye Doyle,

Photo © Greg Naeseth

The current sign outside P. J. Clarke's – 2012

asks for a P. J. Clarke's hamburger while in rehab. The 1990s film *The Insiders*, a true tale about a tobacco company whistleblower, features a cameo appearance by *Daily News* journalist Pete Hamill, standing in front of the mahogany bar at P. J. Clarke's.

If you listen closely to the film you can hear actor Al Pacino say to a reporter, "Let's meet at P. J.'s." The 2006 film *Infamous* also has a scene where actors, playing the roles of the writer Truman Capote and his friend Harper Lee, author of *To Kill a Mockingbird*, are lunching at P. J. Clarke's on hamburgers and beer.

Indeed, P. J. Clarke's Bar has been celebrated in many ways. The November 27, 1971 cover of the *New Yorker* had a drawing of the front bar at P. J. Clarke's by the noted cartoonist Saxon. (The *New Yorker* was founded in the 1920s when Uncle Paddy had turned his saloon into a speakeasy out of necessity.) Later, Leroy Neiman, well-known sports artist, painted a picture of famous customers, including Jacqueline Kennedy, Frank Sinatra, and New York Governor Hugh Carey, sitting at P. J. Clarke's. Other artists produced images of the outside of the saloon that were printed on Christmas cards.

In the Broadway play, *Barefoot in the Park*, the lead character says, "Do you know, in P. J. Clarke's last New Year's Eve, I punched an old woman?" A famous song, "One for My Baby (and One More for the Road)," was composed by Johnny Mercer, while leaning on the bar at P. J. Clarke's. Author Jacqueline Susann mentioned P. J. Clarke's in her 1969 novel, *The Love Machine*. Most recently, the television show, *Mad Men*, a 1960s period piece, featured the Sterling Cooper advertising agency employees enjoying happy hour at P. J. Clarke's.

All over the world people gather in bars and cafés to tell their stories and forget their cares. In Manhattan, bars are important for networking and social climbing—and because most people living in small apartments want to gather elsewhere. P. J. Clarke's is heaven for talkers, their heads bent around tables close together. Even in its early days, my granduncle's saloon offered customers an entry into another world, one of Irish bartenders and portraits of Irish revolutionaries; in the years since, the successive owners have kept the ambiance of the place and built on it. Besides the celebrities, what makes Clarke's bar distinct is that it was not just a bar, but a home. Welcome to the story of P. J. Clarke's.

CHAPTER ONE

Through the Ladies' Entrance

IT WAS A MILD DAY IN OCTOBER 2011 WHEN I APPROACHED THE
East 55th Street entrance of P. J. Clarke's, known as the "ladies'
entrance" in a prior era. I was in Manhattan for my high school
reunion at Dominican Academy on East 68th Street, as well as for
a video interview about my granduncle, Patrick Joseph Clarke,
and his saloon.

Paddy Clarke was an Irish immigrant from the town of
Cloonlaughil in County Leitrim who arrived in New York in 1902,
at age twenty-three. According to my Uncle Joe Clarke, he worked
at the 19th-century saloon, originally designed by beer baron
George Ehret, and saved enough money to buy the place in 1912
from the owner at the time, a Mr. Jennings. Uncle Paddy *may* have
received financial help from a local brewer in exchange for offering

The author as a young girl

a particular brand of beer—many saloon owners sought this kind of assistance. However, there is no doubt that Paddy was a careful, thrifty man, and this allowed him to purchase a business at a time when incomes were very low.

As I opened the dark oak door on 55th Street, many memories returned to me—stretching from the 1940s all the way to the 1970s, when my husband John Molanphy worked here.

In 1943, my heart would beat fast in my five-year-old body when my father approached the side door to the saloon next to the shoeshine stand on 55th Street that had operated since the 1920s. Beyond the stand, where men got their nickel's worth of polishing, were the two steel cellar doors for delivery of liquor and food. In 1902, when Uncle Paddy first worked at the saloon, there were many shops along 3rd Avenue as well as plenty of other saloons, breweries such as Peter Doelger's, and even slaughterhouses. Hundreds of immigrants lived in the neighborhood, and they all liked drinking together and telling stories.

I found it exciting and mysterious to come to this place where my granduncle Paddy reigned. In those days it was the custom for the children in Irish families to accompany the adults to a saloon. Because of Uncle Paddy's rule against women entering and sitting at the main bar, my parents, my maternal grandmother, and I always used this side door on 55th Street—the "ladies' entrance."

Helen Marie with parents John and Helen Clarke – 1941

Uncle Paddy had a reason for his strict rule about where females could enter and sit—he didn't want his saloon to be a hangout for local prostitutes. He wasn't alone in providing a special space for couples; unaccompanied women were not welcome in many saloons of that period. In fact, in the early 1900s, many New York women would not enter a saloon for fear of being labeled a prostitute, because some enterprising Manhattan saloons provided a back room for streetwalkers to meet customers.

Later I learned that this male-only custom at various bars in New York, such as McSorley's, originated in Ireland. Irish fathers liked to take their sons to a bar for their first drink—a rite of passage from boyhood to manhood. In a country dominated by the English, drinking became a symbol of "Irishness" and masculinity. Uncle Paddy's "no women at the bar" rule was simply reflective of the culture at the time. In Ireland these ladies' entrances that led to anterooms for women only were known as "snugs."

This rule at P. J. Clarke's lasted longer than it did at other saloons, but it was changed in the 1960s when several women appeared one day and stood in protest at the front bar. During my visit in October 2011, it was clear that even the saloon workforce had become integrated—there were women hostesses, as well as several barmaids and waitresses.

When I was a child, however, the gender restriction was quite clear, so I would skip through the ladies' entrance and run up to

Uncle Paddy, standing by the bar, welcoming me with his broad grin. I liked older people, especially when they smiled as much as Uncle Paddy did. I felt happy in his saloon.

Moving inside, the darkness of the saloon surrounded us, but Uncle Paddy's brilliant white hair always seemed to brighten the place. After Uncle Paddy greeted us, whoever was behind the bar that day would wave to me. The bartenders were usually burly men with accents that I came to know as Irish—a brogue, my dad told me. Other men holding glasses of alcohol in front of them stood at the mahogany bar with their feet on the brass rail, and they turned toward us with curiosity. The smell of beer hung in the air.

As soon as we arrived, Uncle Paddy dropped a quarter in the jukebox, and the Irish songs began. Then he took our orders— usually ham and cheese sandwiches on rye bread, Manhattan cocktails for the three adults, and a Coke for me. Today P. J. Clarke's has a much more diverse menu that has grown and developed over the years, but still retains that wholesome, down-to-earth flavor.

I remember one particular occasion when, feeling restless after we had finished our lunch, I sidled up to my granduncle.

"Uncle Paddy, do you think you could walk with me into the big bar?" I was fascinated by this area that was off-limits to girls.

Uncle Paddy threw his head back and laughed. "Sure, Marie, let's go."

The whiskey selection at the modern-day P.J. Clarke's Bar – 2012

Photo © Greg Naeseth

Strolling into the front bar, holding my granduncle's hand, I examined the huge beveled-glass mirror at the back of the bar. Then I caught sight of two flags—one was American and the other, which I knew to be Irish, had green, orange, and white stripes. Hanging beside the flags were framed photographs of three smartly dressed men.

"Look at them, Marie. That's Robert Emmet on the left, Michael Collins next to him, famous Irishmen. And you know who the third one is on the right."

"Abraham Lincoln," I said proudly. "And what's that fourth picture with all the writing on it?"

Uncle Paddy chuckled.

"That's the Proclamation of Independence from the 1916 Easter Rising in Ireland."

This was a foreign piece of information. That day Uncle Paddy discovered that my Irish American family had not passed on much of the Irish heritage. He may have already mourned the fact that we did not bake soda bread or learn step dancing—and certainly it was a disappointment that we did not know a great deal about Irish history.

Uncle Paddy was showing his support of the Irish nationalists by hanging the Proclamation of Independence over the bar. The year 1916 was a turbulent one at home in Ireland due to an Easter Monday rebellion against Britain led by Padraic Pearse, James Connolly,

Constance Markiewicz, and many others. But when the British made martyrs out of fifteen leaders, shooting them in Kilmainham Jail without a trial—one of them, James Connolly, wounded and with gangrene, tied to a chair—they set off a strong reaction among the Irish at home who had at first opposed the Easter uprising.

The British executions also horrified Irish immigrants like my uncle who were the most vociferous anti-English voices. The 1916 Irish leader Padraic Pearse once said that without the support of Ireland's "exiled children in America," the Easter Rising could not have taken place, nor the continuation of the rebellion afterwards. Having left their colonized island, these immigrants tended to blame any problem they had on English rule, for they were acutely conscious that the Irish had not gained the same freedom as the Americans who had fought and won their independence from Britain.

Their nationalist efforts also provided the new Irish immigrants with excellent experience in building voluntary associations and writing newspaper editorials and articles. The cause of Irish nationhood bound them together. While Uncle Paddy and my grandparents had lost the solidarity of village life when they emigrated, Irish nationalism became a substitute in their fraternal societies, their newspapers, their lodges, and especially their saloons.

Admiring Michael Collins, a hero of the nationalist movement, Uncle Paddy hung Collins's picture over the mahogany bar, and,

POBLACHT NA H EIREANN.

THE PROVISIONAL GOVERNMENT
OF THE
IRISH REPUBLIC
TO THE PEOPLE OF IRELAND.

IRISHMEN AND IRISHWOMEN In the name of God and of the dead generations from which she receives her old tradition of nationhood, Ireland, through us, summons her children to her flag and strikes for her freedom.

Having organised and trained her manhood through her secret revolutionary organisation, the Irish Republican Brotherhood, and through her open military organisations, the Irish Volunteers and the Irish Citizen Army, having patiently perfected her discipline, having resolutely waited for the right moment to reveal itself, she now seizes that moment, and, supported by her exiled children in America and by gallant allies in Europe, but relying in the first on her, own strength, she strikes in full confidence of victory.

We declare the right of the people of Ireland to the ownership of Ireland, and to the unfettered control of Irish destinies, to be sovereign and indefeasible. The long usurpation of that right by a foreign people and government has not extinguished the right, nor can it ever be extinguished except by the destruction of the Irish people. In every generation the Irish people have asserted their right to national freedom and sovereignty, six times during the past three hundred years they have asserted it in arms. Standing on that fundamental right and again asserting it in arms in the face of the world, we hereby proclaim the Irish Republic as a Sovereign Independent State, and we pledge our lives and the lives of our comrades-in-arms to the cause of its freedom, of its welfare, and of its exaltation among the nations.

The Irish Republic is entitled to, and hereby claims, the allegiance of every Irishman and Irishwoman. The Republic guarantees religious and civil liberty, equal rights and equal opportunities to all its citizens, and declares its resolve to pursue the happiness and prosperity of the whole nation and of all its parts, cherishing all the children of the nation equally, and oblivious of the differences carefully fostered by an alien government, which have divided a minority from the majority in the past.

Until our arms have brought the opportune moment for the establishment of a permanent National Government, representative of the whole people of Ireland and elected by the suffrages of all her men and women, the Provisional Government, hereby constituted, will administer the civil and military affairs of the Republic in trust for the people.

We place the cause of the Irish Republic under the protection of the Most High God, Whose blessing we invoke upon our arms, and we pray that no one who serves that cause will dishonour it by cowardice, inhumanity, or rapine. In this supreme hour the Irish nation must, by its valour and discipline and by the readiness of its children to sacrifice themselves for the common good, prove itself worthy of the august destiny to which it is called.

Signed on Behalf of the Provisional Government,
THOMAS J. CLARKE.
SEAN Mac DIARMADA.   **THOMAS MacDONAGH,**
P. H. PEARSE.   **EAMONN CEANNT.**
JAMES CONNOLLY.   **JOSEPH PLUNKETT.**

The Easter Island Proclamation of 1916, a copy of which hung over the bar at P. J. Clarke's

later, a second photograph of Collins in the ladies'-entrance area. Many Irish shared my granduncle's admiration for Collins, even though Collins was the leader who signed the ignominious 1921 treaty with the British that divided the island into two parts and retained the Irish oath to the English king. Collins was assassinated by the opponents of this treaty, the Irish Republican Army— a death he had predicted when he accepted the British terms. He always explained his signature on the treaty by saying that he did not want any more Irish dying in a war against the British Empire. An ardent opponent of the British, Collins feared a new British invasion threatened by Winston Churchill if the treaty was not signed.

Not far from these framed pictures was a black-and-white photo of Uncle Paddy. In it he was a young man and had dark hair instead of his familiar white mane. He was dressed in a black jacket with a carnation in his lapel, with his black hair parted down the middle and his ruddy face clean-shaven. Under the jacket he wore a starched white shirt and a black tie over black trousers.

"That picture was taken to advertise my bar in the *First Avenue Boys Club News*," he explained.

After gaining ownership of the bar, Uncle Paddy made other changes besides hanging Irish pictures on the walls. He had the now famous "CLARKE'S" painted in gold letters on the front window facing 3rd Avenue, and during the years of his ownership, the bar was known simply by that name. After Paddy's death, the new

Helen Marie with Uncles Ray and Joe Clarke – 1942

owners purchased the use of the name, but the bar became known as P. J. Clarke's, as it is today, though many people refer to the place simply as P. J.'s. Uncle Paddy also changed the white tablecloths, favored by the former owner Mr. Jennings, to the red-and-white checkered ones, similar to those that today cover the old wooden tables in the anteroom and in the 55th Street addition to the saloon.

On my visit to P. J. Clarke's in 2011, I stood at the far end of the bar—it still seemed like foreign territory to me, but I was able to observe the same features that I had noticed as a little girl of five or six. After Uncle Paddy had walked me by the forbidden bar, I felt comfortable repeating the event. When I would get bored with the adult conversation at the table, I would slip off my chair and take a walk by the bar, sliding my black patent-leather shoes along the small, white, octagonal tiles, edged occasionally with black tiles of a Greco-Roman design. I would finish sliding with a flourish and look up at the twenty-foot ceiling, extending through the bar and the front room, made of interlocking tin squares with a floral design stamped onto them. I could see brown spots on the ceiling, which I later learned were caused by tobacco smoke. Moving to the wall, I would run my hand up and down the dark mahogany paneling that stretched three-quarters up the walls.

Many times when I wandered the saloon, the saloon's old dog, Jesse, came running toward me and slipped a little on the sawdust covering the tile floor to absorb spills.

"Good dog, good dog," I told him as I petted him and watched him scamper away.

Now I looked up to see old Jesse stuffed and still at his post over the telephone booth.

On one visit, I became curious about a small window at the end of the bar that overlooked the street.

"What is this window for, Uncle Paddy?"

"That's where people could buy a bucket of beer and take it home to drink in peace," Uncle Paddy said. "The buckets full of beer were handed out through the window to people who ordered from the sidewalk. That way women could pick up the beer for their husbands' suppers. This was before you could buy beer in bottles."

I shook my head, thinking it a very peculiar window. Later I learned that the buckets were called growlers and cost $.25, a charge that even my father's family had to pay.

As a historian, I remembered this conversation with Uncle Paddy and grew curious to learn more about this Irish cultural love of drink. Obviously, immigrants of all ethnicities drank for many reasons—depression, loneliness, homesickness—but historians record that Irish immigrants had additional reasons. They used alcohol to bond together and to show their national and Catholic identity, which helped produce the stereotype of the happy Irish drunk portrayed on Broadway. For some Irish-Americans, drinking at a bar was a way of never forgetting where they came from; these saloons played the additional role of being a clearing house for news and gossip and were a source of contacts, jobs, and loans. At Clarke's, as at other saloons, laborers, lacking money and leisure time, were the steady customers in the evenings.

The Irish bars in New York numbered around 10,000 in 1900 and were usually located on the ground floor of tenement buildings or close to factories and businesses. When Mr. Jennings, the previous owner of Clarke's, purchased the location at 55th Street and 3rd Avenue, he did so because it was on the 3rd Avenue Elevated line where workingmen arrived after their days were finished. This location continued to be a drawing card for Uncle Paddy, but it did not completely explain his success. Some saloons were more popular than others. My father, John, Uncle Paddy's eldest nephew, once explained to me what he thought made Clarke's bar so successful.

"Marie, the saloons that stayed in business had good, quality food and drink and a welcoming saloonkeeper. Many saloons up and down 3rd Avenue set out a free lunch, a spread of saltines, cheeses, salamis, pickles, hard-boiled eggs, and breads. The saltier the food was, the more drink the customers would order." My dad laughed.

"Paddy made a success of his place. He had the time to concentrate on his customers because he was not married. The business was his whole life, and he was always there. None of us ever remember him leaving the place—not even to go to his home in Port Washington on Long Island. That house was just an invest-ment for him."

Bachelorhood was another Irish tradition. At the end of the 19th century, Ireland had more unmarried people and more late marriages than any other country in Europe. Thirty percent of Irish men and 23 percent of Irish women never married. The memory of the 1840s famine, migration, and the Catholic Church's laws on birth control and divorce, along with longstanding Irish poverty, all factored into this late-marriage phenomenon. In addition, older Irish parents expected one unmarried child to stay at home and take care of them.

Uncle Paddy kept up this bachelor tradition in America, and there are no family stories of his having any lady friends. He was so thoroughly married to his business that he had his own living quarters upstairs over the saloon. I laughed when I heard that W. C. Fields, comedian, film star, and famous drinker, once said, "If I had to live my life over, I'd live over a saloon."

Paddy Clarke came down early in the morning to get the bar set up for the day and then stayed very late at night until the last customer left. As a nine- or ten-year-old, I remember my grand-uncle giving off an air of authority, standing behind the bar, keep-ing a safe distance from the happenings around him. He had to be somewhat detached, like a doctor or a counselor, or else he could not have pursued that line of work, which required him to listen to sad tales spun out by people who were not always sober.

Irish bartenders often became amateur psychologists. This is ironic, as Sigmund Freud is reported to have said of the Irish: "This is one race of people for whom psychoanalysis is of no use whatsoever." Freud might have been referring to the idea that many Irish men find it difficult to express their emotions, but have been known to go to a bar and cry into their beers. An Irish friend once told me that if an Irishman feels something, he tends to want to "take something," that is, take a drink.

To use an Irish term, Uncle Paddy was a good publican because he liked to see people enjoy themselves. Fairly gregarious, he wanted to hear people's news and find ways to connect people with one another. Most of all, Paddy Clarke focused on knowing what was going on in the local community. My father told me that part of Paddy's daily routine was to take a walk up 3rd Avenue to get a break from bartending. Wearing his black bowler hat and his best suit, Paddy would stop to visit with other saloon owners on the street. His walk kept him abreast of the goings-on up and down 3rd Avenue.

Besides being a good listener and communicator, Uncle Paddy knew his business. According to my father, at the end of the night, Paddy would shake the liquor bottles, allowing him to tell how much money ought to be in the register. Known to watch his money carefully, he once told a bartender that the bartender was making more money than Paddy himself. Paddy was also firm with customers who had too much to drink, especially if they were verbally abusive or picked a fight. Dad said that if a customer got out of line, Uncle Paddy would retort: "I didn't invite you in off the street, did I?" He usually handled the problem himself with the help of other bartenders or called the sanitation department to collect the inebriates. (The phrase "on the wagon" referred to the water wagons used in New York to carry off drunks.)

Paddy Clarke had many endearing qualities—his eyes were soft, but his jaw was hard. He could remain silent for a long time, and, like other Irishmen, he could be stubborn, but capable of generosity. Uncle Paddy wanted to advance himself economically, yet his bar was his home, and the money he made was not as important as his relationship with his family, his staff, and his customers. While he was quick to bar repeat offenders, he was known to pay for funerals and for poor people's groceries. The heart of the community, Paddy Clarke's bar offered Irish immigrants more than just a place to drink; it was a support network, and if people needed help, the community rallied around those people to do what they could to lend a hand.

A faithful Catholic like the rest of the Clarke family, Uncle Paddy usually attended a late Sunday-morning mass at St. John the Evangelist Church, a few blocks from the bar. He was very proud of his

Catholic heritage and of the Catholic Church's charitable work. Paddy Clarke had arrived in America in a period when there was a huge gap between the rich and the poor, and the Catholic Church played a major social-service role. The Church filled the vacuum in the Irish community left first by businessmen, who emphasized the survival of the fittest, and second, by Protestant charitable groups, who referred to Irish-Catholic immigrants as "refuse." Catholic charities erected schools, hospitals, orphanages, and social-service networks to which Uncle Paddy was known to be a generous contributor.

Nevertheless, when Uncle Paddy applied to join the Knights of Columbus, a Catholic men's religious group, he was turned down because the Knights did not accept bartenders. Paddy tipped his hat to the Knights and, instead, became a member of the First Avenue Boys Club, a men's social group that provided him with contacts in his Upper East Side neighborhood. This gesture revealed that Paddy was obviously a flexible man, and he would need this trait when the country moved headlong into ratifying the prohibition of alcohol through the infamous Eighteenth Amendment to the U.S. Constitution.

CHAPTER TWO

The Second-Floor Flat Over P. J.'s

IN OCTOBER 2011, AFTER VISITING THE MAIN SALOON, I ENTERED a second side door on 55th Street, labeled SIDECAR, and huffed and puffed up the steep set of wooden stairs. Emerging at the top of the second floor, I found myself in a large, elegant room filled with square tables covered with crisp, white cloths sitting on a shiny, wooden floor. Along the exposed brick wall, comfortable, padded benches lined the entire length of the room. The walls were hung with fine pieces of art, and the many windows looked out on New York City streets. Frank Sinatra's voice filled the room. I was in the new restaurant named Sidecar built by Clarke's Group, the owner of P. J. Clarke's since 2001.

I had not been on this level of the building since the 1940s when I visited my granduncle's flat. My fascination with Clarke's bar originated with the idea that my father and his brothers had grown up over this saloon in its solid-looking, red brick, Victorian-era building. In fact, between the years 1916 and 1924, four of the Clarke sons were born there. As I sat at my table waiting to begin the interview with the Irish American organization, I looked toward the front of Sidecar facing 3rd Avenue and remembered tales of my relatives' lives there.

An Irish woman, Annie Moore, was the first immigrant to pass through Ellis Island when it opened in the 1890s; Irish immigrants made New York City the largest Irish city in the world. The census of 1900 revealed that there were 692,000 Irish immigrants living among the three million people of the city. When this number was added to the third- and fourth-generation immigrants of the 1840s famine years, the Irish made up the majority group. This continued for another thirty years until the Irish majority evaporated due to the arrival of people of other ethnicities: Jews, Poles, and Italians.

One day in 1904, two years after Uncle Paddy began working at Jennings's saloon, my grandfather, James Clarke, arrived at 3rd Avenue, tired and worn out from his voyage from Ireland. Uncle Paddy greeted him. "James, brother, *céad mílle fáilte* (a hundred thousand welcomes). Come and sit down, and I'll bring you food and a beer." My grandfather never had such a welcome meal.

In the midst of this large migration to America by people from all over the world, Paddy and James had departed from their small

Grandfather James Clarke – 1911

cottage in Cloonlaughil, County Leitrim, leaving their parents and seven siblings behind. Eventually four other siblings joined them in New York City: Michael, Rose, Annie, and Bessie.

Uncle Paddy told my grandfather that during his first years in New York he had seen remnants of Thomas Nast's cartoons picturing the Irish with apelike qualities, and he had heard about the Know-Nothing political party, strong opponent of Irish immigration. This Anglo-Saxon enmity had its roots in England, where stereotypes of the Irish suited a government that had brutalized the Irish and abolished their language, religion, and land rights.

But, at the same time, Uncle Paddy said that he was encouraged that the Irish were starting to become more accepted in America and that there was less fear of their causing crime or bringing the Pope over to rule. The Irish were creating their own neighborhoods and a network of parishes, unions, and political precincts. Saloons were an important part of the network, as they were the Irish workingman's club. In addition to having these networks, both Clarke brothers had two advantages over other ethnic immigrants: They spoke English, and they were acquainted with the dominant Anglo-Saxon culture of America because of the 800-year English colonization of Ireland.

Even so, there was still antagonism toward the Irish. My grandmother, Mary Mahon Clarke, who also arrived in 1904, told my father about signs in the windows that read: NO IRISH NEED APPLY,

referred to as "NINAs." Sometimes the signs read: ONLY PROTESTANTS
NEED APPLY. It seems that the Protestant householders feared that
Irish-Catholic girls, serving as maids, nannies, and cooks, might
report their behavior back to their priests or secretly baptize their
children. While most people accept this discrimination as a fact of
history, some historians take the view that NINAs were an over-
blown myth. Wherever the truth may lie, prejudice, perceived, or
otherwise, promoted solidarity among the Irish.

Once Uncle Paddy owned his own business, this prejudice
surely influenced him to hire newly arriving Irishmen as his bartenders and waiters and to support the Democratic Party and the
trade-union movement. Like other Irishmen, he bonded with his
kinsmen and continued to send funds home to his family across
the Atlantic. He was even able to take an ocean voyage and visit
them in 1909. By belonging to various Irish networks, Paddy
Clarke found a way to replace what he and his brother James
had left behind in their rural village—a stable social life where
everyone had a role to play under the watchful eyes of parents
and priests.

However, many Americans continued to believe that most Irish
were violent drunks or criminals like Big Tim Sullivan, the political boss of the East Side of Manhattan, or Owen Madden, who was
a highly successful city bootlegger during the 1920s. Uncle Paddy,
as a saloonkeeper, met with special opprobrium—his business was

viewed critically, especially outside of New York. Many Americans knew that large Irish gangs had been associated with saloon life. It did not help the Irish that they continued to celebrate their love of alcohol in song and story—drinking together was a cultural trait of which they were proud, but it did not earn them respect. It is regrettable that at this time few Americans knew of Irish literary and educational accomplishments.

Class distinctions also caused prejudice toward the Irish who arrived from their desperately poor villages without funds—Uncle Paddy came with $5 in his pocket. The Clarkes were poor, but they were literate, unlike many of the 1840s famine-era Irish emigrants. After several years in America, Uncle Paddy joined the Irish who were moving into the middle class. In fact, economics had been a primary motivation for his purchase of the bar, giving him a sense of security and enabling him to be his own boss. There were others, like Judge Daniel Cohalan, Irish American millionaire and militant advocate of Irish independence, who had become wealthy, but were still not accepted by many Americans.

Unlike Uncle Paddy, my grandfather lacked the funds to own a business in New York. After a brief stint working with Paddy at the bar, James Clarke sought a labor job—he had known hard work in Ireland, and he did not avoid it in America. When Grandpa grew tired of bartending, Paddy sent him to the local Democratic Party hall run by Tammany, the group that controlled much of the

Grandpa James Clarke with his three eldest sons John, Joe,
and Jim outside Clarke's bar – 1917

politics and economy of New York City and often used the saloons
to recruit voters.

One Sunday afternoon my grandfather sat next to me, smoking his pipe and recalling that event.

"I sat on a hard bench in the hallway waiting to be called.
Moving inside to an office, the conversation with the ward boss was
easygoing; at first he asked how my brother Paddy was. Then he
followed with questions about where I had lived in Ireland, how
conditions were back home, and if I liked New York. Finally, the
boss got down to business, the business of finding me a job. This
turned out to be an apprenticeship as a steamfitter in exchange for
my support at the ballot box, voting for the Democrats."

Some say Tammany Hall's knack for organizing came from
the example of Irishman Daniel O'Connell, who had succeeded in
regaining rights for Catholics in Ireland taken from them by the
English—property rights, voting rights, and access to education
and jobs. O'Connell did this by a long nonviolent campaign that
involved membership drives and mass rallies and culminated in
the 1829 Catholic Emancipation Act. Tammany Hall might have
emulated O'Connell's method, but it was with a touch of corruption and cronyism. Nevertheless, many immigrants like my grandfather were able to overcome their impoverished circumstances in
America because of the Hall's provision of housing and jobs, much
of which was arranged at the local saloon.

Despite Grandpa James's long working hours, he managed to go to the hall dances sponsored by each Irish county society—Uncle Paddy never did make time to do this, and this may be one of the reasons he remained a bachelor. These societies provided a circle of friends who came from the same part of Ireland and helped keep the Irish informed and united. The Irish made their presence known in their new cities through membership in these societies.

One Saturday night on the East Side of Manhattan, Grandpa met a young woman, also from County Leitrim. Mary Mahon had a soft voice, and Grandpa always remembered her first words to him: "Sure, and I'll be happy to dance with you."

Irish immigrants liked to marry people from their home county, but my grandfather said that he did not care where Mary Mahon came from. Grandpa was smitten after the first dance. From her pictures I know that my grandmother was a beauty with an ivory complexion and gorgeous auburn hair, piled high on her head. She had the smile of an angel and captured my grandfather's heart for his lifetime.

When my grandmother Mary and her sister Alice arrived in New York City, they were assisted by the Sisters of the Mission of Our Lady of the Rosary for the Protection of Irish Immigrant Girls. This organization reportedly helped 12,000 women obtain domestic work. Mary and Alice were, like a great number of the Irish single women—perhaps 60 percent of them—employed as

Grandmother Mary Mahon Clarke – 1911

household servants in Manhattan and on Long Island. It was difficult work, and they were poorly paid, but household employment was safer and offered better benefits than the factories did because women could live on the premises and receive regular meals with their wages. These two Irish girls, who had come from impoverished backgrounds and now worked in mansions, began to dress like ladies and appreciate fine linens and furnishings.

Grandpa James had many a dance with Mary Mahon. Established as a steamfitter, installing heating systems, my grandfather was able to propose marriage to Mary, and the couple exchanged their vows on November 2, 1911. In their wedding picture, a smiling Mary is standing, and a serious James is seated in a chair at her side in the traditional pose. James was thirty-two, and Mary was twenty-eight. Uncle Paddy served a meal at his saloon after the wedding ceremony.

Both my grandparents had saved some money, and Mary ended her work as a housekeeper on 5th Avenue when she became pregnant with my father, John, in 1912. As in other families, money was tight in the Clarke family, but my grandmother did not need outside employment after the children were born, unlike 50 percent of working-class married women in New York City did at the time. While the James Clarkes were not poverty-stricken, they could not have afforded the higher rent of a single-family home.

At first my grandparents lived in an East Side rooming house, but as the family grew, they were invited by Uncle Paddy to share a flat with him in the tenement building housing the saloon on 55th Street. That building dated back to 1868, according to city records, which makes it one of the oldest still in use in New York City. In 1916 my grandparents moved into the second-floor flat over the saloon with my father, age four, and my Uncle Jim, age two. In that four-bedroom, cold-water flat above the bar, Dr. Cooley, a mixed-race physician, was called to deliver four more sons to my grandparents—Joseph in 1916, Thomas in 1918, Charles in 1921, and Raymond in 1924.

The word *tenement* simply meant that someone owned the building and rented it out to as many tenants as would fit. The Tenement House Report of 1900 states that two-thirds of New Yorkers lived in tenement buildings. Since 1898, New York City had included Manhattan, Queens, the Bronx, Brooklyn, and Staten Island, but half of all tenement buildings were in Manhattan. Most tenements were five and six stories high with numerous families, but the one on 55th Street and 3rd Avenue had four stories and sixteen flats—four to a floor.

Families usually paid about $14 for a four-room flat, and this provided a high return to the owner—in some cases as much as 30 percent. As with all other tenements, where the first floor was dedicated to commercial use, Paddy Clarke's saloon occupied the ground floor, with its dark wooden entrance doors facing 3rd Avenue.

Before he died, Uncle Joe Clarke sent me a letter describing his memory of life over Clarke's bar. He said that their home was a cold-water flat, meaning that all water had to be heated on the stove. The building itself was typical of its time, with no steam heat, just a coal stove in the kitchen, and therefore chilly in the winter. Picture the family huddling by the coal stove or using soapstones in their beds for warmth. Because Grandpa James was a steamfitter, he was eventually able to put a radiator in the dining area of their flat and, later, add an electric heater in the front room.

There was no bathroom, just a toilet in the hall of each floor; however, in the slums of the Lower East Side, there were only outhouses. Uncle Joe wrote, "We boys took baths in the kitchen washtubs and dried ourselves alongside the coal stove until we were old enough to go down to the public baths on 54th Street between 1st and 2nd Avenues."

Grandma Mary did her wash in tubs in the kitchen, using a bar of Kirkman's soap and a washboard. As was typical, wash was hung on an outside line stretching between the tenement buildings, revealing the cleanliness of the inhabitants. Lights in the rooms and the hallway were fueled by gas, but later on electricity came to the flats. There was no refrigeration until 1930, so Grandma Clarke shopped every day and sometimes left food out on the fire escape in the cooler seasons.

Uncle Joe wrote that "one of the worst features of our flat was its location by the 3rd Avenue Elevated tracks that masked conversations as the trains roared by. The whole flat vibrated and the floor shook." Even today I myself remember what that train noise was like. There was no chance for any conversation to take place. Uncle Joe said that due to the noise from the trains, as well as from the saloon, my grandmother took her sons on many walks around the city. She especially loved walking up and down Park Avenue and then over to 5th Avenue, where she had first worked as a servant girl after coming to America.

Walking was one of the working-class New Yorker's favorite pastimes, along with going to Central Park and taking an occasional trip to the Coney Island amusement park. Recreation was simple. People enjoyed being out on the street, especially during the hot summers when they spent their nights sleeping on the roofs or fire escapes. The tenement buildings were hot due to the lack of adequate ventilation, and because their flat, uninsulated black-tar roofs captured the heat.

Despite their tight quarters, the Clarke boys had a good time in their building. Once my dad related a story to me about his playing on the fire escapes that were on the side and front of the saloon. He and his brother Jim liked to tip glasses of water over

The Clarke boys with their uncle's new car

the dirty fire escapes outside their bedroom window, and one day the water fell onto a policeman's cap. Dad and Uncle Jim heard the policeman shout as he ran inside up the stairs—terrified, with their hearts beating, the boys climbed off the fire escape back through the window and ran to hide under their bed. Moments later, they could hear the policeman's angry voice at the door, their mother Mary assuring him that she would scold her sons. But my dad told me that when the policeman finally left, she merely rolled her eyes at them, seeing the funny side of their caper.

A while later the same police officer, Tom Quilty, began playing stickball with the Clarke boys and their friends on 55th Street, a form of community policing. Some of the boys who went to school with my father and his brothers wound up in prison, but the Clarkes had great guidance from their solicitous parents, their neighbors, and the Sisters of Charity at St. John the Evangelist Catholic School, escaping the delinquent life. My dad and his brothers had the benefit of a wonderful teacher at St John's school—Helen Bentley, who remained a lifelong friend. A single woman, Miss Bentley arranged frequent parties for the children out of her own funds.

In addition to the austerity of tenement life, another problem was disease. The Tenement House Commission of 1900 reported that tuberculosis (TB) was common due to overcrowding. In 1935, when the fourth son, Tom Clarke, was seventeen, he contracted TB and lost one lung, but he recuperated at Saranac Lake in upstate

New York. Despite the fact that Uncle Tom lived in a very clean flat and that New York City had improved its health codes, he still contracted TB. Tom's experience of incapacitation and recuperation led him to an epiphany—and he entered the Jesuit seminary after his graduation from Xavier High School.

While life over P. J.'s was difficult by today's standards, it was far better than the worst of conditions in New York at that time. There were tenements in Manhattan where conditions were much more severe, especially in the poverty-stricken neighborhoods of the Lower East Side where 500,000 people lived in 1900. This part of Manhattan, with its teeming immigrant population, mainly from eastern and southern Europe, also held many factories, docks, slaughterhouses, and power stations, causing increased air pollution, high noise levels, and obnoxious smells. Mice, rats, and roaches, roaming among the garbage-filled streets, were another danger, and, despite the invention of the electric rail, horses were still kept in these neighborhoods.

These flats were poorly lit, inadequately ventilated, and over-crowded. They were often fire traps. Forty-seven percent of fires in New York City took place in tenements—there were no fire stairways, just fire escapes whose ladders proved difficult for children and older people. Many tenement dwellers were subjected to criminal types, dirty, unsanitary conditions, and loud noise far into the night—dens of violence and misery.

It is clear that the Clarke's tenement at 55th Street and 3rd Avenue was in the better category of buildings—less of a fire trap because it was smaller, not as crowded, with little crime. Uncle Paddy was trying his best to have the flats over his saloon be as comfortable and safe as possible. That is why he had invited his brother James to bring his family to 55th Street and later his sister Annie and her husband, John Grimes, who emigrated shortly after James did. The families in the tenement knew each other and were locals like Pappi, who ran the shoeshine stand, and the Duane family, friends of the Clarkes. It was a very close community. Nevertheless, when Uncle Paddy had enough money to buy the tenement building from the owner, he did not seize the opportunity, declaring, "I can't understand why anyone would want to own a tenement."

But it was the unhealthy tenements that caught the attention of the turn-of-the-century progressive reformers who lumped the whole category of tenements together. These reformers were often members of temperance and religious groups who developed a view that if alcohol were prohibited, life in these tenements would improve. From 1901 on, these progressives did get some improvements made, such as better sanitation due to the newly formed street cleaners who wore white uniforms and were called "white wings." The street cleaners' labor did help reduce disease, as did the fact that water supplies were being tested to guard against water-borne infections.

Helen Hines and John Clarke, Helen Marie's parents, with their classmates on Confirmation Day 1924 at St. John the Evangelist Church

Calls for reform in city conditions where the poor lived came from many quarters.

The wealthy folks were embarrassed by tenement housing and thought it would prove negative to investors. They also feared a popular rebellion. Employers felt conditions in the worst tenements would prevent workers from being efficient. Progressive reformers were concerned that the children of these families might become criminals. City officials wanted the burgeoning metropolis to look prosperous for tourists.

Like the tourists, the Clarkes found New York City an exciting place to live—it was now the largest city after London and was becoming a very important financial hub, as well as a manufacturing center. The spectacular skyline of Manhattan was emerging due to the construction boom beginning in 1900 and lasting for the next thirty years. Prominent in the skyline was the Woolworth Building, with its fifty-five stories, making it the tallest building in the world in 1913. The city planners were tying this large metropolis together—suspension bridges and the new IRT subway system joined the elevated lines, such as the one that ran past Uncle Paddy's bar.

Technology was changing people's lives. The electric streetcar was replacing the horse-drawn carriage, and in 1903, with the invention of the internal combustion machine, the wealthy began driving Packard automobiles through the city's streets. In 1908,

Henry Ford produced the Model T, a much more affordable vehicle, and the Clarke boys began getting rides from their Aunt Rose Clarke Dixon's husband, Jack. Other inventions appeared—the vacuum cleaner in 1901, the washing machine in 1907, the electric toaster in 1909—but it is certain that Grandma Mary did not have any of them in her flat.

The James Clarkes had moved over the saloon during the very year, 1916, of the Easter Monday uprising in Dublin. In November 1927, five years after Irish independence was won, tragedy struck when the six Clarke sons lost their mother to a case of ruptured appendix that turned into peritonitis and then pneumonia. Mary Mahon Clarke was forty-four. My grandmother was not alone, as thousands died of pneumonia and tuberculosis every year, despite New York's attempts to improve health with bacteriological labs, public baths, water chlorination, and pasteurization of milk.

Uncle Joe Clarke wrote that his mother was ever kind and generous and frequently made many of Uncle Paddy's meals and tidied up his room. He said that despite all the stress of living over a saloon next to the 3rd Avenue Elevated train, his mother was a happy person, full of smiles and good humor. One day when Uncle Joe saw her crying—an unusual occurrence—she told him that she was missing her own mother over in Ireland.

When Mary died, my grandfather James was totally bereft and had to be pulled away from her death bed. For years I could only imagine how sorrowful the scene was in the flat over Clarke's bar: six young boys suddenly without a mother and a very distraught husband in shock. Uncle Joe, who was eleven years old at the time of his mother's death, gave me a clearer picture of that day. At the age of sixty, Uncle Joe wrote the following: "I recall the night she died, when Dad came back with the others from the hospital, and (I), hearing the crying of Dad, knew that something was wrong. For months he would cry himself to sleep on a couch in our living/dining room."

As was traditional, my grandmother was waked in her home over the bar, wearing a pair of white rosary beads around her neck. Because she was beloved, many people from the neighborhood came to pay their respects. Grandmother Clarke's funeral mass was held at St. John the Evangelist Church, and her casket was buried at Calvary Cemetery in Queens. I treasure a set of her postcard messages kept by my grandfather until he died.

I never remember any conversations with my father about how he felt after the death of his mother. My dad did tell us, with a catch in his voice, about how sweet his mother was, and he spoke fondly of Aunt Rose Clarke Dixon, who helped take care of the six boys in their flat over the saloon. With the death of his wife, my grandfather became a single parent, and because he was a melancholy man, this took a toll on the Clarke sons, who were more used to their gentle mother.

At the time of her passing, my father, John, was fifteen, and the youngest of the six, Ray, was only three years old. Their mother's death left a hole that no one could ever fill. That was certainly true for my grandfather, who did not remarry and instead mourned his "Molly" until the day he died at the age of ninety-six. As Senator Patrick Moynihan of New York would one day say after the assassination of John F. Kennedy, "What's the use of being Irish, if you don't know the world is going to break your heart?"

While there were many occasions when my grandfather spoke of missing Mary, the great love of his life, he never regretted coming to New York. His sons were raised as Americans. Grandfather James would never answer questions about Ireland—all he said was his homeland was a hard place because of English rule. In those moments we watched his face become distorted and angry. Glad to be in America, my grandfather was like many other Irish immigrants, though some of those other immigrants never got over their homesickness. Grandpa was never actively involved in any New York groups that sent money and weapons to the Irish cause, too busy with his long hours of work and raising his six sons over a bar in the middle of Manhattan.

CHAPTER THREE

City on a Still

"PROHIBITION IS LIKE A BAD COLD; IT WILL GO AWAY." THIS IS what Uncle Paddy often told his family and friends during the period between 1919 and 1933, when the Eighteenth Amendment to the U.S. Constitution made selling liquor illegal. At the time Prohibition struck, Paddy Clarke had owned his bar for seven years, and New York was about to enter the Roaring Twenties.

The Midwestern temperance movement had been gaining strength when Uncle Paddy began working for Mr. Jennings at the saloon. My granduncle had heard about the most famous woman in the movement, Carrie Nation, known as "a female Paul Bunyan" because she was six feet tall and carried a hatchet in her hand to break saloon windows, whiskey bottles, and kegs of beer. Nation once described herself as a bulldog running along the feet of Jesus, and she doggedly ignored being shot at or beaten up by saloon customers, occasionally working in vaudeville shows to pay her hospital bills. Claiming she heard voices directing her activities, Carrie Nation was the most dramatic woman Prohibitionist, but there were also very effective men who led the movement, such as William Anderson and Wayne Wheeler.

During Uncle Paddy's time working as a bartender at the saloon, before he purchased it from Mr. Jennings, the Anti-Saloon League, led by Wayne Wheeler, grew more influential across the nation. The group was very effective at lobbying lawmakers and businessmen to support the Raines Law, which authorized Sunday saloon closings and higher taxes on alcohol. Like other New York bar owners, Mr. Jennings started providing regular meals on Sundays, a service that allowed him to escape the Sunday closing law.

But then the Anti-Saloon League began advocating for the complete abolition of alcoholic beverages and focused on the "evils" of the saloon itself. It was clear from the beginning that the League did not approve of the new immigrants crowding the saloons of the big cities. The Anti-Saloon League originated the Prohibition movement. Members belonged to the "dry" camp; those in opposition to Prohibition were known as the "wets." By 1912 Uncle Paddy was a saloon owner, and he fit the profile of a "wet," a Catholic immigrant living in a large city, voting Democratic. The "drys" did not like his type.

We can only imagine the suggestions and complaints nervous patrons might have popped through the slot during the lead up to Prohibition!

Uncle Paddy read League publications that denounced the saloon for sending youth to their destruction, wasting workers' wages, leading women astray, and corrupting politics. The League put out statistics that said liquor caused one-half of the crime in the country, one-quarter of the poverty, and one-fifth of the divorces. Twenty-two million school children were given temperance education talks three times per week because of the efforts of this "dry" faction, which held that one mere drink could send a youth to dissolution.

One of the biggest complaints of the Anti-Saloon League was that saloons controlled city politics. For a long time many "drys" had made a link between Irish-Americans, alcohol, crime, corruption, and political machines, especially in large cities like New York. It was true that 80 percent of licensed saloons in New York City were owned by first-generation Americans and that many of these owners were also local politicians. Several prominent leaders of Tammany Hall, such as Charles Murphy, had been saloonkeepers.

It was not only temperance folks in the Midwest who opposed the saloon; to many of the progressive reformers of the early 20th century, the saloon was an ugly institution tied to the corrupt Irish political machine. Jacob Riis, the urban sociologist and photographer, said in 1902, "Down the streets, the saloon, always bright and gay, gathering to itself all the cheer of the block, beckons the boys." Riis counted thousands of saloons against just a hundred or so churches in New York. Progressives, like Riis, felt that efforts to make the slums disappear were hampered by the existence of so many saloons.

My father once reflected that Uncle Paddy understood clearly that Prohibition was aimed at extinguishing the saloon associated with the Irish-dominated Tammany Hall and its immigrant clients. He said that Uncle Paddy had bristled at the fact that Frances Willard, a major temperance leader, once denounced immigrants in their saloons as "the infidel foreign population of America."

Uncle Paddy took umbrage at the attack on the saloon. Like the founder of McSorley's, a male-only saloon in Manhattan, Paddy was a churchgoer and did not permit prostitutes or other criminal types in his bar because he had a strong sense of family. Swearing, gambling, and drunkenness were not allowed. Uncle Paddy knew that he was admired as a successful entrepreneur and social bene-factor in the community, having worked hard and risen to respect-ability and middle-class security.

Paddy considered himself not as someone who fed off the misery of the poor, but instead as someone who provided the aver-age immigrant workingman with a place to unwind and celebrate, especially given the impoverished conditions at the time. Paddy Clarke saw his saloon as a club for workingmen. How strongly my granduncle was connected to Tammany Hall politics is unknown. One can only speculate, but because saloons were often the location

Similar to the owner of another Irish bar, McSorley's, Paddy Clarke defended his saloon against the temperance movement's claims that the city's pubs were full of prostitutes and criminals.

for politics he probably had strong ties—Uncle Paddy was a good networker.

It is not known how Paddy Clarke felt about Jimmy Walker, mayor of New York City, who was considered the personification of a "wet." Walker was the new Irishman—debonair, a lover of wine and women, and not one who knew his place. Walker would continue to drink openly during the Prohibition era, frequenting small saloons, like Uncle Paddy's, as well as upper-class clubs. Like other New York politicians, Walker was also corrupt and was finally asked to step down from office by New York Governor Franklin Delano Roosevelt, which he did.

At first, Uncle Paddy thought the Prohibition movement would die out, especially in New York, but then the temperance leaders made clever alliances that proved the cliché that politics makes strange bedfellows. The Anti-Saloon League gained the favor of suffragettes, and this alliance became a huge factor in the growth of the Prohibition movement, as well as in the passage of the Nineteenth Amendment giving women the right to vote. Uncle Paddy was of the old school—women's suffrage was not something he favored, especially after women leaders gave their support to the Prohibition movement.

Eventually, Paddy noticed that Prohibition advocates included others besides the Midwestern temperance people, suffragettes, and anti-immigrant groups. Social worker Jane Addams joined the company of evangelical Christians who were not sympathetic to her work with the poor, but sought her support in opposing alcohol. Uncle Paddy was aghast when the Ku Klux Klan, originally an organization that terrorized African Americans in the South, added Jews and Catholics to their hate list. Because both of these groups were connected to the alcohol industry—many Jews owned distilleries, and many ethnic Catholics were big consumers of alcohol— the Klan supported Prohibition.

John D. Rockefeller donated $350,000 to the Anti-Saloon League, and historians revealed later that his oil interests were a motivating force, because many farm machines ran on alcohol. Henry Ford and other corporatists declared that the country could not run efficiently without Prohibition because they wanted sober employees. Paddy Clarke was upset when some of the labor unions joined their employers in denouncing alcohol. He soon realized that other opponents of saloons had personal interests: Coca-Cola and other soft drink companies, theater owners, and car dealers all positioned themselves as substitutes for alcohol and saloons. Then there were the members of the Republican Party who declared for the "dry" movement and hoped for a chance to divide the Democrats.

As a result of the "dry" campaign, by 1916 twenty-eight states had adopted prohibition laws. Uncle Paddy was very pleased that New York was not among them, because his business was growing and his customers wanted to keep drinking. Like many others, he

never expected that the "drys" could succeed in passing a constitutional amendment banning alcohol, but he became a little concerned when the Sixteenth Amendment to the U.S. Constitution
established an income tax—a tax that could replace whiskey tax
revenue for the federal government.

Historians have written that it was America's entrance into the
European war in 1917, on the side of the British against Germany,
that put the final nail in the coffin of the alcohol industry, the fifth
largest in America. The use of alcohol emerged as a political issue
due to the war fever in the country, with the Anti-Saloon League
making alcohol a national security issue. The League advocated
halting the manufacture of alcohol to conserve fuel and grain for
the war effort and pushed the idea that sobriety was even more
important than it had been before. The federal government's power
had grown during the war, so it was easier for the Anti-Saloon
League to sponsor wartime measures that banned the use of grain
for distillation and gave President Woodrow Wilson the power to
regulate beer and wine manufacturing.

The Anheuser-Busch beer distillery led the battle against these
efforts and gained many supporters. Uncle Paddy joined with
German brewers in the neighborhood in opposing the Prohibition movement. Like them, he was upset when the League became
vehemently anti-German and suggested that German-Americans
were unpatriotic supporters of their homeland. A primary

motive for their accusation was the fact that German-Americans controlled the breweries and beer was the most popular drink in America. Along with their suggestion of German American treason, the League set about making publicity statements suggesting that sobriety for American soldiers would help them defeat the beer-drinking German enemy abroad.

Yet, Uncle Paddy and the wider Irish American community were conflicted—they hated the idea that America would be supporting Britain in the war, especially because the British Parliament had opposed the Irish declaration of independence in 1916. When the "drys" tied Prohibition to patriotism, the Irish-Americans remained neutral on the subject, even though they opposed the proposed law. This most clearly manifested itself when the *Gaelic American*, a New York paper, avoided the subject entirely, while other newspapers in New York City supported Prohibition largely due to pressure from the Anti-Saloon League.

In 1919, when the Eighteenth Amendment was being presented to the states for ratification, Uncle Paddy was very concerned. My grandfather remembered his brother sitting in their flat going over the wording of the amendment: "After one year from the ratification of this article the manufacture, sale, or transportation of intoxicating liquors within, the importation thereof into, or the exportation thereof from the United States and all territory subject to the jurisdiction thereof for beverage purposes is hereby prohibited."

Paddy Clarke's enters a new, drier era.

Grandpa said that Paddy put his head in his hands and turned to his brother.

"James, if this law passes, I am in trouble."

Uncle Paddy spent many restless nights while the supporters of Prohibition rallied in prayer services. Their prayers would be answered, and Paddy Clarke would have to make a big decision.

As soon as the amendment passed, many elites bought up supplies of liquor; Secretary of the Navy Franklin Roosevelt had four cases of Old Reserve delivered to his East Side Manhattan townhouse. There were "liquidation" sales all over town, and people bought alcohol in bulk amounts. June 30, 1919, was called "New Year's Eve in June" because it was the night before the Eighteenth Amendment took effect, and many New Yorkers, in a city now numbering 5.6 million, turned out to get their taste of pre-Prohibition liquor. Clarke's bar was as crowded as the other saloons on 3rd Avenue.

Paddy Clarke had hired extra bartenders that night to handle the crowd. Newspapers were strewn around the tables of the saloon. Headlines said that the Anti-Saloon League had declared that "a new nation will be born," convinced that heaven would come to earth—no more crime, wife beatings, or early deaths from alcohol. On the other hand, some New York papers reported that conservatives were concerned with this build up of federal power, giving more central control over individual rights. Some New Yorkers feared expansion of police powers and loss of civil liberties.

No constitutional amendment had ever taken rights away from Americans. Uncle Paddy, like other bar owners, must have shaken his head. All of these considerations had been raised too late— the opponents of Prohibition had done too little, not believing an amendment prohibiting alcohol would ever pass.

In October 1919, the Volstead Act, which interpreted the Eighteenth Amendment, was passed over President Woodrow Wilson's veto. Wilson said the act was too severe in that it forbade wine and beer as well as hard liquors. Nevertheless, when challenged in the courts, both the Eighteenth Amendment and the Volstead Act were ruled constitutional by the U.S. Supreme Court.

Local brewers on New York's East Side announced that their industry had hoped that Congress would exempt beer and wine, but the "drys" controlled the Congress, and they defined intoxicating beverages as anything with more than 0.5 percent of alcohol. The Volstead Act did allow home production of fruit juice in order to protect the vinegar and hard cider industries and as a favor to apple farmers. Medicinal use was also allowed, and 15,000 physicians lined up for authorization to provide prescriptions for Lydia Pinkham's Vegetable Compound, which was 7.5 ounces of 80 proof whiskey. They would receive many requests for prescriptions in the coming years.

Catholics and Jews were permitted wine for their religious services, though they would have a tough fight keeping this exemption because the Anti-Saloon League was opposed to both groups. Anti-Semitism and anti-Catholicism were rife in many Prohibition circles. The pastor at Uncle Paddy's local parish, St. John the Evangelist, would join other Catholic priests and bishops throughout America in condemning the prejudice in the League's attempts to overturn the exemption.

Thousands would soon be out of work, including brewery employees, bartenders, and grape growers. Meanwhile, Uncle Paddy was considering his options—shut down his bar or ignore the law. He chose the risky path of keeping his saloon open. Other saloonkeepers, fearing a sentence in a federal prison, opened grocery or dry goods stores in place of their bars. There were 15,000 saloons licensed in New York City before Prohibition, 52 percent of which closed between 1918 and 1922. However, numerous "speakeasies" opened. The term "speakeasy" originated from an expression, "speak softly shop," which was a 19th-century English phrase for a drinking establishment that served smuggled and untaxed liquor. The name referred to the fact that customers had to whisper at the door—in other words, speak easy.

Although Uncle Paddy's saloon remained open, it did not meet the definition of a New York–style speakeasy. My granduncle did not install a peephole in the side door, as pictured in movies about the 1920s. His place was not a high-society club for "flappers" and gents dancing to loud jazz music, emptying their flasks of hard liquor into teacups and hoping there would not be a raid by the famous U.S. Treasury agents, Moe Smith and Izzy Einstein. Nor was Clarke's a bare-bones speakeasy hidden in a basement serving poor-quality, high-priced drinks.

Clarke's was more subtle. The bar itself no longer displayed liquor bottles, and only featured a variety of sodas. Regular customers and people in the know were sold alcohol in the side room. Green shades were pulled down, and there were cops on the take. It was an illegal operation, and the whole notion of this period at Clarke's has always been intriguing.

If Uncle Paddy had been a saloonkeeper in a place other than New York City, it might have been impossible to stay open. Paddy Clarke was a shrewd man, however, and he sensed the limited amount of support for Prohibition in his adopted city. New York became an outlaw and from the very beginning did not strictly enforce the restrictive amendment. Nightlife simply went underground. As the prime source of demand for bootleg liquor, New York became widely known as the "City on a Still." This was true despite the fact that federal agents descended on the city and fines and jail sentences were applied. The term *scofflaw* was created during this time, acknowledging that many people were not going to abide by the new proscription against alcohol.

A favorite story of my father's took place during the Prohibition period. One night in 1920, when Dad was eight years old, he was awakened by his six-year-old brother, Jim, who was crying over a bad dream. Dad took Jim down the hall to the bathroom and, on the way back, the boys peeked through Uncle Paddy's half-opened door. As they did so, they could hear a sloshing sound from inside. They opened the door a bit more and saw their Uncle Paddy at his wash basin working with a mixture of different liquids, one of which said "alcohol." Dozens of empty bottles stood ready, and Uncle Paddy had filled other bottles. Off to the side, the two boys could see their uncle's newly installed bathtub filled with more of the curious liquid. The boys later learned that Uncle Paddy was making "bathtub gin"—easy-to-flavor industrial alcohol produced with juniper, glycerin, and tap water.

Uncle Paddy also received weekly supplies of illegal scotch whiskey delivered in a black limousine that pulled up at the 55th Street side of the saloon. He had his men take the boxes and move them down into the sub-basement through the steel doors on the sidewalk. Cups of whiskey would later be served surreptitiously to favored customers.

By one estimate, 2,000 cases of liquor per day entered the coves and bays of Long Island Sound alone. An assistant secretary of the Treasury admitted that his department only seized about 5 percent of all liquor smuggled into the country. When the Mullen-Gage Act was passed by the New York State legislature, the officers of the New York Police Department (NYPD) were delegated to assist the federal agents in enforcing prohibition laws. Most cops did their duty, but some wanted in on the take.

There had been years of police corruption in New York City, much of it condoned by Tammany Hall, whose members were also involved in numerous illegal back-room deals. Investigation followed investigation, but police corruption continued and was given new life during the Prohibition years. It is estimated that cops on the take, often of Irish ethnicity because they represented the majority in the NYPD, made anywhere from $5 a day to $150 a week in bribes from saloonkeepers. Their corruption had the unexpected side effect of limiting the number of alcohol-related court trials, which were swamping the legal system in New York.

One night my father heard a lot of excitement out on the 55th Street side of the bar. He looked out the window and saw a policeman reeling back against the brick wall of the saloon building after Uncle Paddy socked him squarely in the jaw. Dad watched the cop, still clutching his jaw, run away. Later, Uncle Paddy told him that the officer said he wanted more money to look the other way when the big black limousine delivered the scotch whiskey from Canada. Uncle Paddy had refused. I found it amusing that my father, who was at that time a NYPD lieutenant, was telling me about bathtub gin, crooked cops, and black limousines carrying illegal booze.

CHAPTER FOUR

New Beer Day

THE PROHIBITION PERIOD WAS NOT AN EASY TIME FOR PADDY Clarke, even though the odds of a small saloon being shut down were not as high as many of his peers had feared. The federal enforcement bureau was understaffed with poorly paid agents, and they tended to raid the more famous midtown speakeasies so that they could get publicity in the newspapers for their arrests. Uncle Paddy also knew that when the federal agents made arrests in New York, they were hampered by new practices: widespread plea bargaining and reduced sentences from New York City judges whose courts were overloaded with cases.

The NYPD officers often turned a blind eye to saloonkeepers like Paddy, but some did seek a bribe. Local police were required to enforce prohibition laws, but in 1923 Uncle Paddy was elated when the Mullen-Gage Act was repealed by the New York State legislature due to the encouragement of Democratic Governor Al Smith. Thereafter the NYPD was exempt from its enforcement role and could return to arresting more serious criminals. Uncle Paddy felt any possible harassment from the NYPD should end.

Despite this change, there were some New York City saloon owners, who, trying to stay open, were still shut down by federal agents. The upper brass of the NYPD, largely Irish, were often connected with Tammany Hall politicians who opposed Prohibition and had ties to the federal agents. Uncle Paddy was never arrested, nor was his bar shut down. He *may* have known important people in high places.

However, my granduncle did not enjoy acting surreptitiously. Like other neighborhood saloon owners, he wanted to run his business openly. He was often anxious and hoped Prohibition would be a "bad cold that would go away." One day he pulled my sixteen-year-old father aside as Dad was polishing the brasses in the bar. Uncle Paddy let it slip that he was betting on Governor Al Smith of New York to win the presidency.

Al Smith himself had flaunted the prohibition law and served liquor in the Governor's Mansion. Meanwhile, the Democratic Smith was not alone—it was widely known that Republican President Warren G. Harding served liquor at his weekly poker games in the White House. But because of Al Smith's attitude, the "drys"

This way to the dining room – 2012

began to refer to New York City as "Satan's Seat" and acknowledged that they had to be successful in the nation's largest drinking city or their movement would not be viable. The "drys" called for stricter enforcement.

Following Smith's example, when the 1924 Democratic presidential nominating convention was held in New York City, alcohol appeared readily available for the visitors, while "wets" and "drys" argued inside the convention hall. Four years later, in 1928, Al Smith was nominated as the Democrats' presidential candidate, and he authorized a platform that included ending Prohibition. His Republican opponent, Herbert Hoover, did not favor overturning the Eighteenth Amendment, but he called for some modification in the Volstead Act that had implemented the amendment.

Candidate Al Smith acknowledged reality; he knew that by 1927 there were twice as many speakeasies in New York City as there had been saloons before Prohibition—32,000 illegal drinking spots. Indeed, there were 200,000 such places across the nation. Researchers indicate that in the first years of Prohibition, alcohol consumption fell by perhaps 50 percent and deaths from cirrhosis of the liver by 30 percent. But sales of medicinal alcohol (95 percent pure) increased 400 percent between 1923 and 1931. Many Americans began moving from beer and wine to hard liquor because it was actually cheaper to obtain scotch whiskey from Canada than to get beer from illegal American breweries. The high

Inside looking out on an autumn day in Manhattan – 2012

cost of bootlegged liquor was a factor in the decline of drinking during this period, but after the Roaring Twenties got underway, bootleggers, traffickers, and speakeasies grew in numbers, and drinking came back.

The law was being undermined. Hoagy Carmichael was quoted as saying, "The 1920s came in with a bang of bad booze, flappers and bare legs, jangled morals, and wild weekends." He should have added jazz to his list. Some researchers claim that more people were drinking hard liquor in New York than they did before Prohibition.

One day Paddy Clarke picked up his newspaper and read what New York City's Republican reform mayor, Fiorello LaGuardia, had said: "It is impossible to tell whether Prohibition is a good or bad thing, since it has never been enforced." LaGuardia added that to enforce the law would require 250,000 police plus 250,000 more police to supervise the first group. A progressive reformer and opponent of corruption and hypocrisy, LaGuardia announced his desire to see Prohibition ended.

In 1928, Uncle Paddy voted for Governor Al Smith because he was a Democrat and because he promised to repeal Prohibition. There were some Irish, mainly outside the big cities, who distrusted Smith because he was too "uppity," so they voted Republican. Uncle Paddy knew that Smith's candidacy was a long shot—the country was still feeling prosperous and giddy over the Roaring Twenties and many people credited the Republican administrations of Presidents Warren G. Harding and Calvin Coolidge for this "normalcy and prosperity." And when the resurrected Ku Klux Klan added Catholics to their list of enemies and began an ugly attack on Smith's religion, Uncle Paddy became very pessimistic.

In November 1928, Paddy Clarke's morning newspaper announced that the Republican Herbert Hoover had won the presidency by an overwhelming margin. Behind the scenes, pundits wrote that Smith lost because he was a "wet" Catholic and had been attacked not only by the Klan but by an alliance between the "drys" and fundamentalist Protestants. My granduncle chuckled when he read what Al Smith said after the returns were in: "The time hasn't come when a man can say his beads in the White House." Smith, despondent over his big loss in the election, exited politics.

After the 1928 presidential election, the Anti-Saloon League made a big mistake—imagining that Al Smith's huge defeat was due to his opposition to Prohibition, they pushed for a stringent criminal law called the Jones Act. This federal legislation turned Eighteenth Amendment violations from misdemeanors to felonies. Conceivably, a bartender could be sentenced to five years in prison for a first offense. One notorious case of a Michigan woman, sentenced to life in prison after her fourth violation of selling alcohol, made national headlines.

Uncle Paddy sensed that the "drys" had gone too far and that their refusal to compromise would encourage many more people to call for a repeal of the Eighteenth Amendment. He was relieved to read that newspaper publisher William Randolph Hearst called the Jones Act "a menacing piece of repressive legislation," and he was very pleased when the *Irish World* newspaper finally conducted a campaign actively opposing the prohibition laws as a loss of freedom.

A year after Herbert Hoover was elected president, the country faced another crisis. Uncle Paddy, like most investors, lost a great deal of money when the stock market plummeted. New York City was hit hard in 1929. Fortunately, Paddy Clarke was thrifty and his bar had gained new customers, so there was never a threat of bankruptcy. For one thing, some of New York's more famous restaurants, such as Delmonico's, had been shut down due to Prohibition and, as a result, neighborhood saloons like Paddy's gained customers. Uncle Paddy continued to stay in business through the economic downturn despite the fact that multitudes of New Yorkers were out of work—the Wall Street crash had hit all sectors of society. Perhaps that drove people into the speakeasies in greater numbers.

Paddy Clarke began to notice that more middle-class customers were frequenting his bar, and these New Yorkers told him that they resented Prohibition as a loss of freedom. They became an important group advocating for its abolition. The elite had flaunted their consumption of illegal alcohol from the very beginning,

A well-stocked bar at modern day P. J. Clarke's – 2012

stocking their clubs and homes with large amounts of liquor before the law went into effect and buying on the black market afterward. The working class resented Prohibition as a personal assault on their ethnic traditions and as a deep imposition on their lives. They expressed their anger to Paddy Clarke, annoyed that the elite appeared to be above the law.

When halfway into his term, President Hoover, a Quaker who hated alcohol, authorized the Wickersham Commission to look into the effects of the Eighteenth Amendment, Uncle Paddy felt there was a chance of repeal. In 1930 this Commission pointed to the corruption and dereliction of duty among the federal revenue agents and also to the success of organized crime elements in replacing businessmen bootleggers and undercutting the law. Paddy Clarke was cautiously optimistic when President Hoover announced that the states, not the federal government, should decide whether they would maintain Prohibition, which the president referred to as a "noble experiment." Uncle Paddy hoped that New York might act, but Hoover failed to move the process along.

Despite Hoover's lack of leadership, the movement to end Prohibition gained weight for several reasons. As Paddy Clarke could attest, people liked to drink, and in New York City, the fact that alcohol was illegal somehow made it more sophisticated. The "drys" had counted on New York closing down its drinking establishments, but the "City on a Still" had only created more of them.

At the passage of Prohibition, Paddy Clarke had decided that its laws were largely unenforceable and that his laboring-class customers would never support it. He was right.

Uncle Paddy heard that in the small towns of America, the use of a medicine made from Jamaican ginger extract, known as Jake, was being widely used. Jake was 85 percent alcohol and was legal, but because it was often contaminated with chemicals to stretch out the quantity of the solution, the result was a poisonous "Jake leg." In the cities, bootleggers were stealing industrial alcohol, and, overreacting, the government ordered poisons to be added, killing 1,000 people in New York alone. The resulting deaths in cities and small towns helped produce a backlash against Prohibition.

Businessmen joined in, claiming that Prohibition had inhibited their trade—people seemed to go out less, and the entertainment industry protested. A plus for Uncle Paddy and the movement to overturn Prohibition was the fact that movies were popular, and drinking by actors and actresses on the silver screen helped make alcohol more acceptable again.

But Paddy Clarke was growing impatient. He could not understand how the American people could keep such an unpopular and unsuccessful law on the books. When it became clear that the murder rate had doubled due to alcohol wars between organized crime syndicates, Uncle Paddy asked his fellow saloonkeepers when

Americans would understand that Prohibition was devastating and that evil men were benefiting economically.

Then Uncle Paddy got some help from a surprise quarter. Many mothers who had supported Prohibition watched their teenage daughters and sons criminalized as they rode around in automobiles, drinking from flasks; these women began calling for the law to be overturned. A leading New York City socialite and Republican spokeswoman, Pauline Morton Sabin, campaigned very effectively for the end of what she considered the corrupting and ineffectual prohibition laws by bringing people from all political persuasions and classes into her fold. Historians hold her up as one of the principal leaders in the fight to end Prohibition. Women had been one of the largest forces in the passage of the Eighteenth Amendment, and, after they got the vote with the Nineteenth Amendment, they became active politically, as well as socially, flocking in large numbers to the new speakeasies for cocktails and cigarettes. Now they would lead the repeal of Prohibition.

As the economic depression deepened, the hard times became the final catalyst that led to the passage of the Twenty-First Amendment, just as World War I had been the event that encouraged the passage of the Eighteenth Amendment. In those difficult economic times, many businessmen favored legalizing and taxing alcohol, possibly decreasing their own tax liabilities, while government agencies also saw an opportunity for increased revenues if legalized alcohol were taxed. Paddy Clarke realized a tax on alcohol would affect him, but it was well worth it to have Prohibition ended.

Uncle Paddy cheered when Democratic presidential candidate Franklin Delano Roosevelt announced that he advocated the complete repeal of the Eighteenth Amendment. During his 1932 campaign Roosevelt claimed that the law was a failure and that the U.S. Treasury would gain hundreds of millions of dollars from legalizing and taxing beer alone. Roosevelt's opposition to Prohibition worked and, along with the horrific economic conditions in the nation, helped him win his overwhelming victory in 1932; if this man stood against the government's legislating private morality, the people approved of him for the presidency.

After Roosevelt's election, Uncle Paddy was hopeful that the ban would be removed, and to his delight the president immediately signed an executive order restoring beer and wine to legal status. With the country deep in the Great Depression, FDR was reported to have said that "it was a good time for beer," and the first case of post-Prohibition beer was delivered to the White House by a team of Clydesdale horses. In New York City, thousands gathered for "New Beer Day." The federal government reported that on the first day when beer was legalized again it collected $10 million in taxes.

Soon, New Yorkers would have that beverage for breakfast to celebrate the repeal of the Eighteenth Amendment. Uncle Paddy was surprised that Prohibition ended as quickly as it did when, in

April 1933, the Twenty-First Amendment to the U.S. Constitution was passed and Section 1 read simply as follows: "The eighteenth amendment to the Constitution of the United States is hereby repealed." Michigan was the first state to ratify and Utah the thirty-sixth state, thus giving the necessary two-thirds approval. This action revised the role government would play in moral reform and offered a note of hope that perhaps the economic situation in American would improve.

On the day of the passage of the Twenty-First Amendment, Uncle Paddy smiled as new and old customers packed his place. When the Eighteenth Amendment was passed, Uncle Paddy had read the words of Secretary of Navy Josephus Daniels: "The saloon is as dead as slavery." The country, in which the Puritans had built a drinking place before they built a church, proved Daniels wrong. Americans did not like their personal morality legislated; drinking had gone on during Prohibition, and now it would continue legally. Paddy Clarke's "bad cold" was cured.

Between the deliveries of whiskey that arrived on the shores of Long Island from Canada, Uncle Paddy's mixture of gin, and his supplies of the legal 1 percent "near beer," Clarke's customers had made it through the Prohibition years. Uncle Paddy was a survivor; he had trafficked illegally in alcohol, but had escaped punishment. On the day Prohibition ended, pedestrians passing by Clarke's bar saw a sign posted: FAREWELL TO THE 18TH AMENDMENT.

CHAPTER FIVE

New York's Finest

WHILE CUSTOMERS HOBNOBBED AND DRANK DOWNSTAIRS, AN IRISH family had struggled through the day-to-day challenges of the times upstairs. The James Clarke family lived over Clarke's bar until 1937, when my grandfather, retired on disability from steam-fitting, moved with four of his sons to a rental house in Woodside, Queens. My father, John, was married and living nearby, and my Uncle Tom was in a Jesuit seminary. When my grandfather heard where his sons had relocated him, he said, "Woodside, my God, you can't even get a beer out there!" Despite their move, the family continued to have strong ties with Uncle Paddy and his saloon.

The difficult Prohibition period had ended with Roosevelt's election, but the Great Depression was still crippling the nation. It was 1935, in the midst of the Depression, when my father joined

1935

Strolling Down 5th Ave.

Daily News Photographer

Helen and John Clarke in the Easter Parade, New York – 1935

the NYPD. The next year he married his childhood sweetheart, my mother, Helen Hines, on October 17. Grandpa Clarke told him that he was too young at age twenty-four to get married, and Uncle Paddy concurred. The Irish married late. A very handsome couple, my parents were captured by a *New York Daily News* photographer as they were walking up 5th Avenue in the Easter Parade of 1935. My mother looked like Greta Garbo's sister, and my father resembled Cary Grant. Uncle Paddy pinned up the picture behind the bar.

My mother always recalled that Uncle Paddy had offered Dad money to attend college, but he said he wanted to go to work— no more schooling for him. But obviously Uncle Paddy must have been very fond of my dad. A generous man himself, Dad took on the task of keeping Paddy's financial books after he moved out of the flat on 55th Street. Many Sunday afternoons when we visited the saloon Dad would leave us to go downstairs to do this work. While he was gone I would wander to the front bar, where the Irish bartenders treated me royally. Once I heard Dad tell my mother that he would not accept any money from Uncle Paddy for his time on the books.

There were times when my parents reminisced about Dad's first job out of high school, working in 1930 as a draftsman in Stamford, Connecticut, hoping to study architecture. They wondered what might have happened if he had not given up drafting work in order to have the security of an NYPD payroll check. The term, "New York's Finest," had its origin during the Great Depression because so many of the men who joined the NYPD at that time had good educations and fine credentials; the economic times were too difficult for them to utilize their trade, college, and law degrees.

My father had many different posts with the NYPD. He was a desk sergeant in Brooklyn, a fingerprint expert, a lieutenant in lower Manhattan, and a "shoofly," an officer assigned to see if the patrolmen were on task. He hated this last duty. One of the effects of Dad's police career with its odd work schedule was his limited opportunity for social associations. This contributed to the fact that his brothers were always his chief friends.

Growing up, as the eldest son, Dad had assumed a great deal of responsibility for his younger, motherless brothers. This pattern continued through his adult life, and I was always struck by what a good big brother he was. For Dad, people were more important than money. His attitude did not happen by accident and shows the influence of his elders. Dad and his brothers, who lived over P. J.'s, were all "New York's Finest."

In 1942, after the attack on Pearl Harbor, there was a Christmas sendoff for Charlie Clarke at Clarke's bar as he departed for army maintenance school and eventually for action in the Pacific. From family conversations I can reconstruct this event. All the Clarkes were gathered around the front bar, and Grandpa Clarke looked very worried. His third son, Joe, was already posted as

John Clarke, new officer at the New York Police Department – 1936

an army instructor at a base in the States. A few months later, his youngest son, Ray, received his draft notice and had to give up attending Manhattan College. Ray was also headed for the Pacific Theater.

The night of the sendoff for Charlie, Uncle Paddy said, "James, you need to stay brave and be glad that all your sons are not going to war." My dad's occupation as a police officer was protecting him from the draft. Uncle Tom was studying to become a Jesuit priest, and all religious men were exempt from fighting. As a New York City fireman, Uncle Jim did not have to serve in the armed forces, either. Jim had affiliated himself with the Catholic Worker House in lower Manhattan, started by the famous pacifist Dorothy Day. Under her influence, Jim declared himself a conscientious objector, but it was his fireman's job that protected him from the draft.

Before he died, Uncle Joe sent me a packet of letters he had saved that were written to him by my father when Joe was in the army. These dozen letters penned between December 1942 and April 1943, when Dad was thirty years old and Joe was twenty-four, are an example of my father's brotherly concern, in this case for Joe's health as he advanced through army officer training school in New Jersey. Dad wrote: "Joe, we want to send you whatever you need—Helen and her mother have made a large care package for you." Dad always ended his letters to Joe by saying how lucky the

1935

Jim Clarke, at the New York City Fire Department ceremony, standing with John Clarke, Helen Marie's father – 1935

people on the home front were. He lived his life with a good deal of gratitude, as did his brothers. Luckily, all three sons who went to war returned home safely.

In the middle of his life, Dad became especially close to Uncle Joe Clarke who was a charming man with excellent business acumen. He was selfless in his devotion to his family, his clients, and his employees, as well as to the extended community, serving on several charitable boards. Of all the Clarke sons, Joe appeared to have the deepest attachment to Irish culture and song, having absorbed it during his years over the saloon.

When Dad had narrowly missed the acceptable score on the civil service exam to become a police captain, he decided to retire from the NYPD at age forty-three. He eventually became employed at his brother Joe's firm, New York Roofing Company, as the supervisor of the roofing crews and later as an accountant for the company, a position he held until his death in 1982. Dad always said that Uncle Joe was the best boss any man could have.

Dad also had a special relationship with his brother Jim, who was two years younger and my godfather. Uncle Jim remained a NYC fireman until he decided to enter the Capuchin Franciscan seminary and become a missionary priest to Japan. This was a surprise to many members of the family as Uncle Jim liked girls and he loved to pull funny stunts. But his idealism, surely picked up

Helen Marie with sister Joan and brother Jack at ordination of
Father Tom Clarke S. J. – 1950

from his family, from the Sisters at St. John the Evangelist School, and from his association with Dorothy Day at the Catholic Worker House, led him to join the priesthood.

Every three years Uncle Jim, now known as Father Martin de Porres Clarke, came home from Japan to New York on a three-month's leave of absence. He was so beloved by his former colleagues with the New York City Fire Department that they organized a "Bucket Brigade" and raised funds for his mission in the poverty-stricken Ryukyu Islands of Japan, where the U.S. Okinawa naval base dominated. A large fireman's boot was placed on the bar at P. J. Clarke's to encourage customers to make contributions to Uncle Jim's mission. It was my father who took care of the funds donated to Uncle Jim. Dad would come home from his job and go immediately to his desk and start writing thank-you notes to the various donors. In this way, Dad was united with Uncle Jim and his work in Japan.

Uncle Jim made the *New York Times* front page when he was instrumental in getting the Japanese government to accept a Vietnamese boat family—the only time Japan allowed this to happen. Jim loved the Japanese people, and, while he did not succeed in baptizing many, he was very happy that he helped them get decent housing and health care. Always proud of his family and their simple life over the bar, Jim died in New York City in 1995 after serving there for several years as a hospital chaplain. As he aged,

Uncle Jim's face became riddled with laugh lines—he was the chief comedian in the family, but his brother Charlie was a close second.

Uncle Tom, the Jesuit priest, was away a great deal from New York City, but he stayed very close to my mother and father by mail. As the most brilliant brother, Uncle Tom could fill a book listing all his accomplishments as a writer, theologian, and retreat director, but all the Clarkes would agree that his epitaph could best have been "He loved his family." Uncle Tom was ever proud of his Irish origins, and he made visits to both maternal and paternal relatives in Ireland. Dad liked to recall the day when some of his younger brothers were playing on the stairs at the saloon and they rolled their brother Tom down to the basement and thereafter always laughingly claimed that the bump on his head was what made Tom so smart.

Despite living above a saloon, only one of the Clarke boys, Charlie, followed Uncle Paddy into the bar. Returning from World War II, Charlie took on the role of manager for Paddy and then remained the manager until his retirement in 1989. I have fond memories of joining my dad and Uncle Charlie for a night at the Roosevelt Field "trotters" racetrack—we would place a bet at the $2 window and, if we won, the money would go toward pizza after the races. After Uncle Paddy's death and the sale of Clarke's bar in 1948, Uncle Charlie's warm welcome was the major reason we continued to visit 55th Street, the term my family used to refer to the saloon. His sense of humor will long be remembered by his seven children and by hosts of customers and employees at P. J. Clarke's.

And, finally, there is Uncle Ray, my only uncle still alive, who always appreciated how good my father was to him. Living in Flushing, New York, as a widower, Ray is cherished by his children and grandchildren. He had two careers in his life—as a detective and then with special services at the NYPD, guarding important visitors to New York. Later Ray served as the chief of security for RCA at Rockefeller Center.

A favorite story of Uncle Ray's was the time when he was standing with his father, James, at the bar at Clarke's. A drunk was giving his brother Charlie, manager of the saloon, a very hard time. All of a sudden Grandpa Clarke, who had muscles from steamfitting, reached over and hit the man with one arm. The inebriated man was knocked over, and that was the end of the trouble for Uncle Charlie that night.

Ray and his wife, Mary, had a very happy marriage and opened their home to many, many people. On Sunday mornings, all the married uncles would bring their children to Uncle Ray's house, where he would cook breakfast and Aunt Mary would charm all of us with her warmth. My dad loved playing with all his nieces and nephews who numbered nineteen in all, plus his own three children, making a total of twenty-two grandchildren for Grandpa

Clarke, several of whom worked part-time at P. J. Clarke's during their college years.

Before he died, Dad gave me his impression of life over P. J.'s. He said he never forgot his origins in that saloon, sitting next to the 3rd Avenue Elevated line, where he had enjoyed the kindness of his mother, the camaraderie of his brothers, the dedication of his father and uncle, the fellowship of people at the bar, and so many happy family gatherings. Throughout his life, Dad was a devoted Catholic like his Uncle Paddy and his parents; he was egalitarian in his approach to people, accepting them for who they were, something he picked up from being around a saloon.

CHAPTER SIX

The Little Bar That Could

WHEN I WAS TEN YEARS OLD AND A FIFTH-GRADER, MY FATHER told me that Uncle Paddy was dead. It was April 1948 and my granduncle was sixty-nine years of age. I can remember exactly where I was standing in the room I shared with my three-year-old sister Joan, whose godfather was Uncle Paddy. We were living in our two-family, semidetached house in Jackson Heights, Queens. Joan and I each had a twin bed and a chest of drawers at the foot of our beds; the window of our room looked out onto a small garden with a honeysuckle-covered metal fence. When my father appeared at the doorway and told me the news, I teared up. My father gave me a big hug and held me tight. I looked up at him.

"Oh, Daddy, I really loved him."

Dad nodded his head.

Gravestone for Clarke family at Calvary Cemetery,
Queens, New York

"Marie, your mom and I are going to Manhattan for Uncle Paddy's wake."

Suddenly all I could remember was the day Uncle Paddy had told me about his American Wake as he left Ireland—the traditional party his family gave him because they never expected to see him again. My dad and I had walked down a dark hall on the second floor over the saloon, and then Dad stopped and knocked on one of the doors. Uncle Paddy answered. "Marie and John, come in—it's good to see you."

As soon as I walked into the flat, I could see that Uncle Paddy had very few furnishings—a white, iron bed with a mattress on a spring board next to a plain, wooden, four-drawer dresser. A large, leather-like chair with a matching footstool sat by a black, metal standing lamp. When I looked around, I saw that the floor was covered with grey, speckled linoleum and that there was a large double-hung window in the middle of the room. Off the main area was a small kitchen with a double sink and a set of burners on top of the adjacent counter; next to this was a doorway leading to a toilet and a large bathtub on legs.

Uncle Paddy indicated that Dad and I each should sit on the metal kitchen chairs.

"Marie, how about a glass of milk and some cookies?"

Uncle Paddy opened the icebox.

I nodded, and as he poured milk into my glass, Uncle Paddy began talking.

"Your father and his brothers lived with me in a larger flat until your grandfather retired and moved out. I miss them. They're my family, not having children of my own."

Uncle Paddy opened a box of Oreo cookies and put two on a plate near my glass of milk. Then he got up and poured my dad and himself glasses of beer from a bottle sitting on the counter. He sat down and raised his glass to my father.

Then I saw that Uncle Paddy's eyes had suddenly misted over.

"We all came to New York thinking we could do better." Uncle Paddy smiled to himself. "On the day before I left Ireland I sat in the Gortleteragh parish house. I bowed my head while Father gave me his blessing. He said that all the best young people were leaving Ireland. Every one of us who left the parish had to hear his lecture about the evils of New York City. Listening to Father, I knew that nothing he said would change my mind—I was sailing on the next boat for New York because I wanted to make something of myself."

I remembered looking at Uncle Paddy with a frown on my face.

"What do you mean, Uncle Paddy?"

"Marie, I did not want to be poor anymore. I was the first Clarke to leave and five of my brothers and sisters came to America after me. Even my brother Michael, the eldest male of the nine of us, and the one who inherited the family cottage, left for America after years of trying to work the poor soil. God bless him—he was killed in an auto accident here. Only three of them stayed behind— John and Catherine and Lizzie."

Uncle Paddy paused and took my hand.

"Around eight o'clock on the night before I left, I stepped out into the yard to begin my last party at home, my American Wake."

I looked at Uncle Paddy, puzzled.

"Why do you call a party an American Wake?"

"In Ireland a wake is a special occasion you have when a person dies—it goes on for days and is a celebration of their life. An American Wake is a bit like that. No one really dies, but going to America was like dying as it was such a long way. My family never expected to see me again, but I surprised them and came home for a visit after a few years."

I nodded my head with new understanding as Uncle Paddy continued.

"Neighbors had brought food and drinks to add to what my family had set out in our garden. By the end of the night, my father was drinking too much and my mother was crying with the other women."

Uncle Paddy paused a moment. I could sense he was deep in his memories.

"Then the Farewell Reel began. It started out as a lively tune, then got very sad. The Reel told me that my American Wake was over and that I should collect my bag and say good-bye to my family."

Uncle Paddy looked at me and smiled.

"I have never regretted leaving Ireland."

When I finished my milk and two Oreo cookies Dad and I said good-bye to Uncle Paddy and walked along the dark hall again. My eyes had opened wide that day, listening to Uncle Paddy tell his story of his American Wake—I thought that he must have been very brave to leave his home.

I came into understanding Irish history and my heritage late in life, but the seed was planted at Clarke's bar, where Irish history decorated the walls. During a 1970 trip to Ireland, the tales I had heard from my granduncle Paddy became real, especially as I was able to visit County Leitrim where he was born. Sitting in the Parochial House (rectory) in his hometown, I realized that I might be in the very same room where Uncle Paddy had visited his priest to get a blessing for his passage to New York.

Years after his death, I learned that my granduncle could be quite tough with people, even though he had a good heart. He had enjoyed his life at his saloon, but like some of the Clarkes, he had a certain melancholic air about him. To the Irish, death is a release from life that is seen as long and hard, a "vale of tears," as they say.

A well-known citizen, Paddy Clarke had his obituary notice published in the *New York Times*.

Clarke, Patrick J. April 23 at his residence 915 Third Avenue. Native of County Leitrim, Ireland. Beloved brother of Mrs. Annie Grimes, James F. Clarke, Mrs. Elizabeth Skelly, Mrs. Thomas K. Breen, the late John, Michael, Mrs. Rose Dixon and Catherine. Funeral from Plaza Funeral Home 40 W. 58 Street Tuesday 10:15 Solemn High Mass St John the Evangelist. Interment Calvary Cemetery.

Times had changed since my grandmother Mary Clarke's death more than twenty years before—Uncle Paddy was waked in the Plaza funeral parlor, not in his flat. His place was too small, and so many people wanted to pay their respects. Paddy Clarke had created a publicity ad for customers when he joined the Third Avenue Saloon and Bartender Association. On the top was his name, address, and telephone number: P. J. CLARKE, 915 THIRD AVENUE; TELEPHONE — 1609 PLAZA. Below was his picture and below that a rhyme. This ad was displayed on a table in the funeral home. It read:

Miles' Cream Ale shall never fail to quench a thirsty throttle,
The imported wines are very fine to make the weary frisky,
But there is nothing made that can compare or equal Clarke's whiskey,
As they all say Clarke's for good whiskey it is a household expression and a family suggestion
To beat Clarke's whiskey is out of the question
With a Patrick Henry Cigar.

Uncle Paddy left no will—he had told my father that wills only invited the grim reaper to come sooner, an old Irish superstition. The absence of a will meant probate court and the sale of the saloon business and Paddy's home in Port Washington, Long Island, where the younger Clarkes had enjoyed so many happy summer days. My father was the person who facilitated this transaction with the help of an attorney, a lengthy process that wore Dad down. The absence of a will also meant that New York State took a large part of Paddy Clarke's estate in taxes. The remaining proceeds were divided among twenty or so relatives, some of them living in Ireland.

In 1948, the new owners of Clarke's bar, Italian immigrants and antique dealers, Mr. and Mrs. Daniel Lavezzo, Sr., appeared on the scene. The couple was well-dressed—the husband in a suit and tie, the wife with a hat, purse, and gloves—and both with lovely manners. As they took possession of the bar and its Clarke nomenclature, they decided that the saloon would now be known as P. J. Clarke's. The Lavezzos were happy to have my uncle, Charlie Clarke, continue as manager because he had worked closely with Uncle Paddy for several years. In turn, Uncle Charlie said he always found Mr. and Mrs. Lavezzo to be pleasant and supportive.

The Lavezzos, who already owned the building where the saloon was located, purchased the adjacent building on 55th Street, expanding the restaurant space. More red-and-white tablecloths

Clarke brothers with dates and friends at a Port Washington, Long Island, beach house owned by P. J. Clarke – 1933

were ordered, along with dozens of old-fashioned steam-bent chairs to be placed around eighteen wooden tables.

The new owners traveled regularly to Italy to find old treasures for the large furniture showroom that they built over the back room of the saloon. Thick carpets covered their showroom floor, where an eclectic mixture of 17th- to 19th-century Italian antique tables, chairs, couches, and candelabra was displayed. The front-area flat where my granduncle, my grandparents, and my father and his brothers had lived was turned into office space. The Lavezzos hired Roslyn, a middle-aged single woman, to be their office manager and bookkeeper. Roz, as she was known, ran the business when the Lavezzos were in Italy. She also worked with Uncle Charlie on keeping track of the P. J. Clarke's accounts, including a very select group of charge customers.

Uncle Paddy would have been surprised by these changes in the saloon, as well as those in the neighborhood. More businesses had moved uptown, and the advertising crowd was frequenting P. J. Clarke's. Uncle Charlie said that customers liked the ambiance of the place, its physical location, and its inexpensive, tasty food. The menu at the saloon was being extended by the Lavezzos— now you could get delicious bacon cheeseburgers that became the favored item on the menu, veal scaloppini, steak tartare, and beef stew, along with New York–style cheesecake and hot apple pie with cheddar cheese, all at a very reasonable price. When the number of customers increased, Uncle Charlie, as the manager, hired even more Irish bartenders and waiters, lending an authentic aura to the place.

In 1952, I had begun high school at Dominican Academy on East 68th Street, near Park Avenue. Across the street from our Academy was an elegant home owned by Dorothy Kilgallen and Dick Kollmar, radio commentators on the show *Breakfast with Dorothy and Dick*. Coincidentally, the couple had a regular table at P. J. Clarke's bar for interviewing and prerecording their guests. Designed for privacy, table 38 was a secluded, round, oak table surrounded by three walls in an alcove. There was a telephone jack and an outlet for the radio equipment for Dorothy and Dick's "studio." The couple's program, foreshadowing television talk shows such as *Live with Regis and Kathy Lee*, included charming chit-chat each morning with celebrities around Manhattan—people from Broadway, the arts, and the media. It was customary for the couple to be alerted by P. J. Clarke's staff when a celebrity came to the saloon—Dorothy and Dick could zip over in a taxi from 68th Street to 55th Street and interview the person.

After her husband Dick's death, Dorothy Kilgallen, a slim, elegantly dressed woman with a distinctive, clear voice, continued to be a frequent visitor to P. J. Clarke's. Moving out of radio, she became the most famous syndicated female print journalist of her day. Kilgallen also appeared as a panelist on the television show, *What's My Line?* and she started bringing some of her mystery guests to Clarke's, one of whom was Harry Belafonte, an instant convert to the saloon. In the 1950s Kilgallen was assigned for a year in England, where she became privy to the highest levels of English society, as well as the British intelligence community. She would utilize these connections for her journalistic work until her death in the 1960s.

As we advanced in our high school years, my Dominican Academy classmates and I were eager to socialize in Manhattan. The law at the time allowed eighteen-year-olds to imbibe, and although most of us did not turn eighteen until 1956, in 1955 we were definitely engaged in barhopping. One time, my Uncle Charlie, manager of P. J. Clarke's, saw me coming out of the East 54th Street Brew House with one of my friends. He proceeded to wag his finger at us, because he knew we were underage. When we came to P. J. Clarke's for a meal, Uncle Charlie was ever-vigilant to ensure that we did not order any alcohol.

After turning eighteen, I had my first legal drink at P. J. Clarke's bar. That night Uncle Charlie filled me in on some of the happenings at the saloon, where the doors opened at eight o'clock in the morning and closed at four o'clock in the morning. The crew just threw out new sawdust on the floor each day. My uncle related that the new owners, the Lavezzos, had a son, Dan Jr., a burly man with rugged good looks who was a natty dresser, frequently wearing a madras plaid sports jacket.

Dan Jr. loved to mix with the celebrity crowd at P. J. Clarke's and tended to sit at a table in a quiet alcove near the entrance to the back dining room so that he could meet and greet. He understood that being successful in the restaurant business demanded attention, and he was heard to say that he "ate up the energy at P. J. Clarke's where customers could enjoy both anonymity and intimacy." This anonymity was extended to celebrities, and Dan Jr. went out of his way to see that Clarke's was not mentioned in the gossip columns so that celebrities would feel protected at his saloon.

Dan Jr. was bringing the sporting world to Clarke's; he gloried in the fact that prizefighters Jake LaMotta and Joe Lewis came to his table. Rocky Graziano became a customer and always insisted on sitting under the autographed picture of himself. Soon the New York Yankees baseball players were customers along with Dan Jr.'s favorite athletes, the New York Giants football team, whom he regularly treated to free drinks after their games on Sunday evenings. Uncle Charlie said that when the Giants came in, all the staff knew whether they had won or lost by their demeanor—in either case, the players liked to drink a lot, but if they had lost there were arguments over who was responsible for the mistakes. They were a noisy, garrulous group, and they welcomed the saloon's closing time of four o'clock in the morning, as did the theater folks who came after the curtain fell on their performances. Word of the ambiance of P. J. Clarke's spread, and many journalists and media folks, as

The world famous ambiance at P. J. Clarke's – 2012

well as Hollywood celebrities, began to stand at the bar, two or three deep. Uncle Charlie said that there was a story to be told every night.

One of P. J. Clarke's frequent customers was Elaine Kaufman, later to be the founder of her own popular bar, Elaine's[1]. A short, heavyset woman, Elaine hung out with Dan Jr. and was encouraged by him to start her own place. Restaurant owner "Toots" Shor was in P. J. Clarke's the night Elaine met with Dan Jr. to discuss her idea for a restaurant that she hoped would act as a "salon" for writers and other creative types. Toots told Elaine that she could be his successor, but Elaine modeled herself after Dan Jr. Her restaurant at 88th Street and 2nd Avenue became a tremendous success and Dan Lavezzo Jr. provided the inspiration. In later years Dan Jr., so proud of his own food menu and the friendly ambiance at P. J. Clarke's, commented that people did not come to Elaine's to eat, but to find out how they rated. Dan Jr. said he would have found hosting such a place exhausting; he preferred relaxing at his table and having celebrities pass the time with him. Ironically, when Elaine died and her bar was up for sale in 2011, Clarke's Group considered bidding on it.

When she opened her place, Elaine hung a greeting on the wall of her bar—a statement by English author Samuel Johnson

---

1. *Everyone Comes to Elaine's: Forty Years of Movie Stars, All-Stars, Literary Lions, Financial Scions, Top Cops, Politicians, and Power Brokers at the Legendary Hot Spot*, A. E. Hotchner (Harper Entertainment), 2004

extolling the merits of tavern life. Johnson had opened saying that "there is no private house in which people can enjoy themselves so well, as at a capital tavern." Johnson went on to list the reasons for this: freedom from the anxiety of having to please guests, waiters who do a better job than servants because they are hoping for a good tip, and the fact that customers know they are welcome. The English author could not have described the attraction of a good saloon in better words.

A second pub owner whom Dan Jr. helped start in the bar business was Joe Allen. Allen was a frequent customer at P. J. Clarke's, and one day Dan Jr. suggested that he take a job as a waiter. Allen says that this idea to work at Clarke's proved to be "magical." He loved serving the celebrity customers at Clarke's, which he described as "a grimy place—dark, exposed brick walls, probably not painted since the First World War, the menu on a chalkboard on the back wall, the same dark, mellow feel that eventually predominated at . . . my first restaurant." Allen once said that "if someone were in the headlines during the day they would be at Clarke's that night," a tribute from a future tireless saloonkeeper and restaurateur. By 1959 Allen felt he had enough experience to open his own saloon on 3rd Avenue and 73rd Street, which many say was a clone of P. J. Clarke's, including the red-and-white checkered tablecloths.

Dan Jr. tried to talk Allen out of opening his place, telling him it was very risky and that his own success at Clarke's was a fluke.

In fact, Allen revealed that Dan Jr. got very angry and shouted out that 75 percent of new restaurants close in five years. However, the rest is history. Joe Allen, having been trained by Dan Lavezzo, went on to create an empire of eight saloons, including several abroad in Paris, London, and Toronto. While Elaine's was frequented by writers, Allen's had a special place for dancers. Clarke's customers were far more eclectic than the clientele at either one of the saloons Dan Lavezzo had spawned.

Joe Allen had always loved the fact that many connections were made at Clarke's, and during one of my visits, Uncle Charlie described how movie actor Ernest Borgnine and stage star Ethel Merman had announced their marriage at P. J. Clarke's in June 1958; however, their union lasted only two months. In contrast, rock and roll singer Buddy Holly had proposed to Maria Elena Santiago at P. J. Clarke's only five hours after they met, but their marriage lasted until his death. Holly wrote the song "True Love Ways" for Maria Elena as a wedding gift. In April 2011, Clarke's hosted a "true love ways" event, and Maria Elena unveiled the photo of herself kissing Buddy Holly at their wedding. Today this picture hangs over their original table.

While Buddy Holly was proposing to Marie Elena, I was finishing my first year at Marymount Manhattan College on East 72nd Street near 2nd Avenue, a subway ride away from P. J. Clarke's. To supplement my scholarship at the college, I took a part-time job at the Bonwit Teller's department store on 5th Avenue and East 57th Street, near Tiffany's and the Plaza Hotel. I could run over to P. J. Clarke's for a quick lunch on Saturdays and exchange stories with Uncle Charlie. I, too, had a few celebrity tales to tell, having seen actresses Kim Novak and Audrey Hepburn both purchasing clothing at Bonwit's. I did a lot of gaping at these two beautiful women—I still marvel at how celebrities have to get used to this, even when they are dining at P. J. Clarke's.

Despite our academic schedule, my Marymount College friends and I made frequent forays to the saloon, mainly for an early dinner. It was clear to me that my granduncle's bar had grown into a popular watering hole, sophisticated and no longer only a local hangout. While I continued to enter P. J. Clarke's through the "ladies' entrance," the situation had changed for women in general. Uncle Paddy would have raised his eyes at the number of women gathered around his front bar. It was Dan Lavezzo, Jr. who had broken the rule of "no ladies' at the bar" when one afternoon a group of thirty determined, unaccompanied women ordered drinks at the front bar. Dan Jr., dashing off to the racetrack, waved aside objections from the bartender, and Uncle Paddy's traditional rule was history. The little girl who had begged her granduncle to let her visit the men's bar has never stood at P. J. Clarke's front bar, but has always sat in the back room, though I do remember coming in the front door with my husband, John, on a few occasions.

Grandpa James Clarke seated between sons Father Tom Clarke S.J.
and Father Jim Clarke OFM Cap. Standing behind them are Ray,
Charlie, Joe, and John Clarke – 1960

And then, one day in 1965, I picked up a newspaper and found an article with a headline saying: "Tishman Company buying up the block between 55th and 56th Streets on Manhattan's East Side." In 1955, the 3rd Avenue Elevated train, the last of its breed, had been torn down and, without this obstruction and noise, the price of real estate along 3rd Avenue went through the roof. In the 1960s the Tishman Real Estate Development Company began buying up the whole block around P. J. Clarke's to facilitate their plans for a forty-seven story office building with Marine Midland Bank as the anchor tenant.

Tishman wanted to buy out the owners of P. J. Clarke's and level the building, but when company executives approached the Lavezzo family they were told that the building and the saloon were not for sale. The Lavezzos did not want to give up their antique and restaurant businesses, even though by selling they would have made a tremendous profit on their investment. Negotiating with Tishman was tough, but the Lavezzos held their ground, unlike all their neighbors on 3rd Avenue between 55th and 56th Streets. They were assisted in their efforts by notables all over Manhattan, including Johnny Carson and Ed McMahon, who waged a long, drawn-out public relations battle to save P. J. Clarke's. Important customers urged the owners to campaign for historical-landmark status. Landmark preservation laws were passed after the old Pennsylvania Station was torn down to make way for the

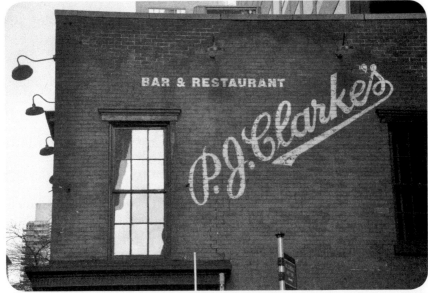

Still standing in 2012

new Madison Square Garden, and these laws helped the cause of Clarke's bar.

Finally, to get their project going, Tishman agreed to buy the Lavezzos' property for $1.5 million, with the arrangement that the Lavezzos owned the saloon business and would lease the entire building for ninety-nine years. As part of this agreement, the top two stories of the tenement that Uncle Paddy never wanted to buy were torn off the building and were traded for air rights to allow the high-rise next door to be more visible. This was an extraordinary piece of engineering, and many members of the Clarke family made comments such as "P. J. would never have believed this."

Clarke's bar was considered a historical landmark; the little red-brick Victorian-style building surrounded by office high-rises struck the passersby as a step backward in time. My granduncle Paddy's place became known as the "little bar that could" because it had avoided demolition from the East Side Manhattan office development. In effect, because of their determination, the Lavezzos had enshrined Paddy Clarke's place—one of the saloons that had survived the Prohibition years.

CHAPTER SEVEN

Lost Weekend

A MAGICAL EVENT HAD OCCURRED IN 1944, DURING THE WAR YEARS, while Uncle Paddy was still alive. The film *The Lost Weekend*, about an alcoholic writer, had featured Clarke's bar in some of its scenes. In 1958 I was studying the Prohibition period in my American history class and, coincidentally, alcoholism in my psychology class at Marymount College. The combination of the two subjects provoked me to think.

One afternoon I took myself to Clarke's, where my jovial Uncle Charlie greeted me as I walked through the side entrance on 55th Street.

"Marie, let's get a table in the back room. The owners have been fixing up the place, and we've got a brand-new kitchen just completed. But we are keeping the chalkboard as the menu. I have some time, so I'll eat an early supper with you."

After we had been served our Cokes, along with bacon cheeseburgers and fries, I asked Uncle Charlie whether the filming of the *The Lost Weekend* had been due to the saloon's speakeasy history.

Uncle Charlie shook his head.

"It really had to do with the fact that Charles Jackson, the author of the book, *Lost Weekend*, was one of the saloon regulars, and he recommended Clarke's to Billy Wilder, the director of the movie version. I knew Jackson—his book is semiautobiographical because he was an alcoholic himself; he got into drinking when he was a TB patient in a Swiss sanitarium. After seven years, Jackson began a recovery and wrote his novel about this alcoholic writer who goes on a weekend binge."

I was intent on every word, even though I had never read Jackson's book nor watched the movie. I decided I would do both very soon. Uncle Charlie went on to tell me exactly how it had all come about. He had heard the story from Uncle Paddy many times.

"Marie, one day Paddy is on duty behind the bar. In walks Wilder, a short, stocky man. He puts his foot on the brass rail and orders a cup of coffee from the bartender. Paddy is busy setting up the liquor bottles on the shelves. Wilder tells him that he is meeting Charles Jackson, so the two of them can discuss the filming of his book."

Glassware ready to be filled at modern day P. J. Clarke's – 2012

Photo © Greg Naeseth

Uncle Charlie paused and took a sip of his Coke.

"Paddy watches Wilder light a cigar and begin studying the saloon, checking out the pictures above the bar. It is nine o'clock in the morning. Suddenly, the 3rd Avenue train races by right on time, and Wilder almost jumps out of his skin. He calls out to Paddy, 'How often do these trains go by?'"

"Paddy responds: 'Every ten to fifteen minutes.'"

"With that Wilder slams down his coffee cup and curses: 'God almighty, why didn't Jackson tell me?'"

Uncle Charlie chuckled.

"Now Paddy's curiosity is up—when author Charles Jackson arrives, Paddy hears Wilder and Jackson begin talking. Wilder says: 'Jackson, I have spoken to my partner Charles Brackett, and he is eager to write the screenplay for your book. Brackett has two alcoholics in his family, his wife, and his daughter, and he says he is going to write an Academy Award winner. We'll pay you $50,000 for the rights. Do we have a deal?'"

Hearing this, I was amazed at how quickly decisions can be made in Hollywood and I listened intently as Uncle Charlie continued with the story.

"Jackson beams and shakes Wilder's extended hand. Then Wilder takes a hard look around the bar and continues talking. 'The trouble is I really like this saloon; I like the look and feel of the place. It's a perfect setting for the story—the dark wood gives a gloomy feeling. But the bad news is the train noise. Jackson, let's take a walk over to Sardi's. I'll buy you a meal and we can put our heads together about the situation.'"

Uncle Charlie shook his head.

"It's amazing what happened next. Jackson told Paddy how Wilder had come up with an idea to solve the problem of the train noise. He said Wilder smashed his cigar in the ashtray and his eyes lit up. 'That's it. I'll have the studio build a facsimile of the bar. Paramount has a good crew of engineers; they can come to New York and study the architecture of the saloon.'"

And that was exactly what happened. With Uncle Paddy's permission, Paramount Studios built Clarke's bar right on their set in Hollywood. In the film the bar's name was Nat's, not Clarke's. It was reported that actor Robert Benchley walked daily onto the Hollywood set and ordered a shot of bourbon, just as if he were on 55th Street and 3rd Avenue. Benchley, a noted New York writer who grew up a teetotaler, had turned to booze during Prohibition and died of cirrhosis of the liver shortly after *The Lost Weekend* was filmed.

After talking with Uncle Charlie, I watched the movie and read about its filming. Wilder's staff found a suitable midtown apartment to be used as the home for the main character and arranged for the use of other sites in the script, such as the Metropolitan Opera and Bellevue Hospital, as well as assorted rooming houses and restaurants not far from Clarke's bar. English actor Ray Milland accepted

A screenshot from The Lost Weekend, *showing the noisy Third Avenue El in the background.*

the leading role of Don Birnam and Jane Wyman assumed that of Birnam's girlfriend, Helen. Filming began immediately, but many scenes had to be shot with hidden cameras after New Yorkers began interrupting the filming to get autographs from Milland.

Milland once described his experience of making *The Lost Weekend*. The actor went on a diet of dry toast, coffee, and grapefruit before the filming began in order to appear as a man who had forgotten to eat because he only enjoyed drinking. He lost eight pounds. To further understand the role, Milland spent a night in Bellevue psychiatric ward, where he put on hospital pajamas and got into bed. Fifteen alcoholic men in the ward gave him a taste of reality. Many had held successful roles in advertising and politics; others were from the Bowery, but all of them had delirium tremens. Milland wrote about the gross smells, the moaning, and the crying of the men.

The Lost Weekend appeared in 1945 and represented one of the quickest transformations from novel to screenplay in Hollywood history. In England the film was called *The Lost Weekend: A Diary of a Dypsomaniac*. The critics loved it; the movie received the top academy award, Best Picture, even though other excellent pictures, *Spellbound*, *Bells of St. Mary's*, *Mildred Pierce*, and *Anchors Aweigh*, were also nominated. *The Lost Weekend* also won Best Director and Best Screenplay, and the Best Actor award went to Ray Milland for his role as Don Birnam.

When Milland took this part, he was advised by his agent that it could be career suicide. Billy Wilder, on the other hand, had predicted that whoever played the lead male role would get an Academy Award, and he was right on the money. After the awards night, Wilder and Brackett were greeted by liquor bottles dangling from the windows of their Hollywood studio, just like the main character, Don Birnam, had outside his apartment in the film.

The Lost Weekend was controversial and could easily have been shelved. When the liquor industry heard of Wilder's film, they offered Paramount Studios $5 million not to release it. While Paramount turned the liquor industry down, Billy Wilder laughingly said he would have accepted the money if it had been offered to him. Ironically, temperance groups also opposed the movie because it showed so much heavy drinking and depicted alcohol's conferring transient feelings of superiority, clarity, and creativity, which could make drinking enticing to young people. Despite the temperance groups' initial opposition to the film, *The Lost Weekend* was judged an important public message movie about alcohol addiction. Birnam, himself, says to the bartender: "It shrinks my liver, doesn't it, Nat? It pickles my kidney, yeah. But what does it do to my mind?" The bartender remarks that, for Birnam, "one drink is too many and a hundred not enough."

On the day we sat together talking about the filming of the *The Lost Weekend*, Uncle Charlie wound down his story by confiding some details about Uncle Paddy. Besides complaining to Uncle Charlie about fans of the film coming to his bar, there was one issue about the *The Lost Weekend* that really upset Paddy Clarke. The novel and the movie both include a prostitute character who frequents Nat's Bar looking for customers. The actress playing that part happened to be Billy Wilder's mistress at the time. In the film, the prostitute and Don Birnam are mere acquaintances, but Birnam, in a happy moment, offers to take her to dinner.

As a good Irish Catholic and responsible bar owner, Uncle Paddy did not admit prostitutes to his saloon; it was a major reason for the "ladies' entrance" on 55th Street and for his ban on women standing by the bar. He had deep reservations about a prostitute appearing in what viewers of the film believed to be his bar.

Uncle Paddy may have been bothered by this scene, but *The Lost Weekend* would begin to make Clarke's bar one of the centers of media and celebrity life in postwar Manhattan. It would never be the same neighborhood saloon again. When Paddy Clarke left County Leitrim, he was a young Irish farm boy looking to improve his lot. He stepped off the boat with little money in his pocket, but he had a lot of determination, and his new city was booming— Uncle Paddy had worked hard to make a success of his bar, and luck began to make his place famous. It is a terrible shame that after a lifetime of hard work, three years after the film premiered, he died.

A long way from the Big Apple and the lights of Hollywood, the original Clarke family cottage in County Leitrim, Ireland, as it appeared in 1989.

CHAPTER EIGHT

Birds' Eye View

IN THE STRANGE WAY THAT LIFE TWISTS AND TURNS, MY HUSBAND worked on two occasions at Clarke's behind the bar where Uncle Paddy had started off all those years ago. In 1960, when Uncle Charlie hired my then-boyfriend John Molanphy to work days while John attended Fordham University at night, Charlie and John clicked. Uncle Charlie's wonderful presence and sense of humor were a huge part of the ambiance of P. J. Clarke's, and he and John were a good match in their ability to see the funny side of situations and to enjoy the numerous characters among the staff.

There was O'Brien, the old Irishman who restocked the bar from six o'clock to ten o'clock each morning—grizzled, with long, stringy hair, he left the saloon each day with a bottle of Seagram's Seven Crown in each of his baggy overcoat pockets. A short, fat,

John Molanphy, Helen Marie's husband, with employees behind the
bar at P. J. Clarke's – 1962

cigar-chomping jukebox man came in once a week with his key to unlock the machine's cash box. Moe would empty the big pile of coins onto table 3 in the front room and he and John would begin counting. Moe always told John stories about his many other stops where people tried to slip coins under the table—he said that never happened at P. J. Clarke's.

There were Frankie Ribondo and Jimmy Ennis who manned the door skillfully and profitably, placing customers at selected tables. Frankie had an early interest in New York architecture and had worked since age fourteen in the Lavezzo family antique business— it was the senior Lavezzos who hired him to work the door at the back room. Jimmy, a graduate of Andover Academy, began his employment at P. J. Clarke's to pay off his bar bill and stayed thirty years. Only good tippers got the attention of these two men. Stories abound about Frankie and how determined he was to earn big tips. One night Lord Carrington, former British foreign secretary and NATO secretary-general, and President Giscard D'Estaing of France were cramped into adjoining tables, while Frankie held back a big table for a favored customer, a local New York politician.

John reported that the waiters and bartenders did very well from the tip cups that were placed next to the registers and that the men were certain to give a hard time to customers who did not tip well, whereas good tippers were treated royally. One waiter, Paddy Baker, received a huge tip from a customer who knew Paddy had six kids. John was especially impressed by barman Tommy Joyce's ability to encourage customers to tip big—some nights Tommy would stand at a particularly wealthy customer's table giving him full attention. The other waiters cooperated and handled Tommy's other tables, knowing he would put a big tip in the cup for all to share. Unfortunately, greed got the best of one of the older bartenders, and John remembers the day when the man was found with purloined tip money falling out of his pockets. The older waiter was banished from daywork to night work, where the men on duty gave him a hard time. He quit Clarke's soon thereafter.

John enjoyed the company of all the employees at P. J. Clarke's, but he especially liked the staff who kidded around. We have a picture of John with three of the daytime staff wearing hats behind the bar because they were defying the superstition that it was bad luck to do so. One of the men in the picture is Pete Cerino, a former champion bantam weight boxer and a friend of Rocky Graziano, who often came to visit P. J. Clarke's when Pete was on duty doing maintenance work, such as keeping the mirror behind the bar sparkling clean. Pete's face and body revealed his prior career, but he had a great heart.

One of the other men in the picture is German American Walter Potzrebie, who was the short-order cook running the grill across from the bar. He and his friend Frankie Neugebauer, a maintenance man who took care of the menus on the chalkboard, had served in the German Merchant Marine and were captured in New York when World War II began. They were placed together in a detainee camp in Nebraska, and after the war they were able to become U.S. citizens and live in New York. On one occasion John Molanphy helped Frankie return to East Germany for a visit. The Communist government required a statement from American police that Frankie did not have a criminal record—John took Frankie to the 51st Street Police Precinct to get the documents signed, where a very puzzled desk sergeant complied.

The third person in the picture is Mike Murphy, who, along with his brother Dermot, was "straight from the auld sod," as many of the bartenders were. The Murphys often opened the bar in the morning and did not stop cracking jokes and pulling stunts until they left. Other staff included Italian brothers Angie Baio, a handyman, and Charlie Baio, a day waiter, who were like Mutt and Jeff in appearance. Charlie had an eye for the ladies and would exclaim over the beauties who walked into the bar. John had a running dialogue with Irish bartender Phil Rafferty, who favored the lunchtime models from the agencies on the East Side.

This interesting group of waiters and staff were supervised by Charlie Clarke. John described my uncle as clever and caring, but strict. John said that Charlie prepared the weekly schedule for the men by penciling in their hours on large sheets of green graph paper. The schedule was thumbtacked to a corkboard on the wall inside the back door leading to Charlie's downstairs office, but it could change if Charlie needed to discipline a bartender or waiter. Suddenly a shift or two would be erased. John said Charlie was wily and never revealed what day he would come to work, keeping everyone on their toes. The boss would come in at any hour and work different locations—behind the stick at the bar, in his office, or on the floor waiting tables. Charlie was firm, but he always treated everyone fairly and had their respect.

In addition to enjoying the staff, John was fascinated by the pageant of characters who arrived to eat and drink at P. J. Clarke's. There were supermodels, stockbrokers, journalists, athletes, men in tuxedos, women in gowns, cops in plain clothes, tourists with their Bloomingdale's shopping bags, salesmen complaining about their bosses, and drunks looking disheveled. One could see people from all levels of society watching and being watched. Often customers could barely squeeze inside the door, and the bar was three deep. John said that more and more tourists were coming to the saloon, mainly in the daytime, making it hard for the local folks from the advertising agencies and media networks to get a table.

At any time of day it was not unusual to see plainclothes police detectives from the local 51st Street Precinct hovering at the bar. Their presence offered Uncle Charlie and George the bouncer backup support for dealing with any troublemakers. The custom was for the police to have a free meal and to leave

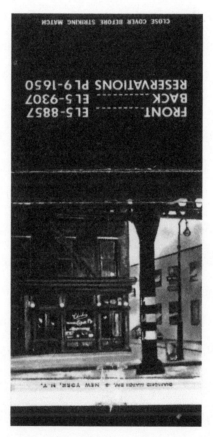

A vintage matchbook from P. J. Clarke's earlier days when patrons could smoke at the bar.

a quarter as a token payment. This cop-friendly atmosphere meant that none of the Mafia types came to P. J. Clarke's—no numbers racketeers or loan sharks could do their business there. Uncle Paddy would have been pleased.

John would tell me lively stories about the various celebrities who frequented the saloon. Humphrey Bogart liked to stand at the bar, enjoying his scotch. Frank Sinatra always ended his nights in Manhattan with a bourbon and water at P. J. Clarke's after enjoying dinner at Sardi's and stops at two other bars, Jilly's and Jimmy Weston's. Sinatra was at the peak of his career and in ruddy, good health. He had given up his pork-pie hat and sports jackets from the 1940s and now wore well-tailored, expensive suits with Hermès neckties from Paris. He had ended his smoking habit to preserve his voice.

And speaking of voices, there were nights when Louis Armstrong would sit with Sinatra, and his gravelly voice could be heard over the din of the back room, though Armstrong mainly liked to come to P. J. Clarke's in the early morning and play his trumpet. Armstrong was thrilled when Sinatra gave a benefit show at Carnegie Hall for Martin Luther King, Jr. The jazz artist appreciated the role Sinatra was playing in the desegregation of Nevada casinos and hotels, by refusing to entertain at certain hotels that were still discriminating against African Americans.

The word among the waiters was that Sinatra believed that he owned table 20, but they didn't mind, as Frank was a very good tipper. Sometimes the whole Rat Pack—Sinatra, Sammy Davis Jr., Peter Lawford, and Dean Martin—appeared together. Peter Lawford was the most composed of the group, while Dean Martin was the most boisterous, followed closely by Sammy Davis. The Rat Pack mingled with the players from the New York Giants football team, going over the night's game, just won or lost. On other occasions George Steinbrenner, the owner of the Yankees baseball team, joined the Rat Pack at their table.

Uncle Charlie supported the Lavezzos' policies, and he instructed the bartenders and waiters not to make a fuss about celebrities and to protect them from customers seeking autographs. No pictures were allowed. To nosy customers the waiters would say, "These folks are customers just like you—they want respect and privacy." This was true even when Marilyn Monroe entered the bar through the 55th Street side door, always on the arm of an elegantly dressed, prosperous, older man. The woman who had starred in *How to Marry a Millionaire* appeared to carry her role over into her dating life.

Marilyn frequently wore her favorite color, baby blue, and her gowns were usually strapless and made of gathered satin, draped in layers around her body. Sometimes she wore a printed silk scarf, tied under her chin in the Russian babushka style. John said that Marilyn never took off her dark glasses until she was seated at her table. If you were close enough to hear her speak, she would vary her tones between her sultry femme fatale and her squeaky, little-girl voice.

Sometimes Marilyn was joined by her good friend, Truman Capote, who loved to dance with her in supper clubs around Manhattan before coming to P. J. Clarke's. Lee Strasberg, her dramatic coach from the New York Actors Studio, would bring Marilyn to the saloon after she had given a performance at the studio, where her goal was to become a great actress.

On any night that Marilyn came to P. J. Clarke's, there was an audible gasp from both customers and staff; however, the waiters always composed themselves and stood ready to seat her and her date in the most private table available. She always ordered a split or a full bottle of champagne, depending on her date's tastes. When Marilyn died in 1962 from an overdose of drugs mixed with champagne, the waiters at P. J. Clarke's shook their heads—they knew of her taste for the bubbly.

While Marilyn Monroe was wining and dining around New York City, I was a senior at Marymount Manhattan College. In 1961, I decided to join a group of fellow students and march in the St. Patrick's Day parade—a parade run by the Ancient Order of Hibernians, an all-male society. This parade brings big crowds to every Irish bar in New York City. A cousin of the Clarke family, Jack McCarthy, was the announcer at the parade for more than forty years.

At the end of the parade I made my way over to P. J. Clarke's, where my boyfriend John was on duty. The queue for the already crowded bar was around the corner, all the way down the street. As was usual on March 17, the police from the 51st Street Precinct had erected wooden barriers all the way down 3rd Avenue to 56th Street to prepare for the block-long crowd that would gather around the bar. The people who stood in line for hours just wanted to say that they had a beer at P. J. Clarke's on St. Pat's Day. Inside no green beer was served—Uncle Charlie never considered this custom an option. Customers, crushed together at the front bar, were encouraged to leave after their first round so that others could have a taste of the draft beer. Just as on any other day, drunks were escorted out, and tipsy folks were declined service and asked to leave.

In Ireland, St. Patrick's feast day is celebrated as a religious holy day for the patron saint, followed by family gatherings. Not so in New York City, where turning out on St. Pat's Day had long been a mechanism for showing Irish-American solidarity, as well as the Irish's newfound prosperity and political power. Unfortunately, drinking to excess was also part of the parade goers' agendas.

The native Irish hate what we've done to their religious holiday and find it very demeaning; being drunk, they say, should not be the same thing as being Irish. After all, Ireland is known as the

"Land of Saints and Scholars." However, there is an Irish poem that goes like this:

> *St. Patrick was a gentleman*
> *Who through strategy and stealth*
> *Drove all the snakes from Ireland,*
> *Here's toasting to his health;*
> *But not too many toastings*
> *Lest you lose yourself and then*
> *Forget the good St. Patrick*
> *And see all those snakes again.*

Uncle Paddy was named for Saint Patrick, a Celtic Briton, once a slave in Ireland and then the bishop who converted Ireland to Christianity without any violence. St. Patrick came to love those fighting, drinking people who enjoyed storytelling and had previously placed their spiritual needs in the hands of a pagan group known as the Druids. The poem above points to the fact that several Irish saints, Patrick, Brigid, and Columban—all promoted the use of alcohol in their churches and monasteries. The Irish tolerance for alcohol goes way back and the 9th-century Viking invasion only increased it.

While I never had a beer at P. J. Clarke's on St. Pat's Day, I did enjoy a brew on other occasions. In the 1960s, whenever I came to the saloon to visit with John and Uncle Charlie, I followed the old custom and walked through the 55th Street "ladies' entrance" to sit at a table. Sawdust was still sprinkled on the white tile floor, and Jesse, the stuffed dog, stood atop the telephone booth near the ladies' room. Jesse, a stray, had been Uncle Paddy's dog, and the story goes that Jesse was very intelligent. Uncle Paddy would send the dog across the street with a nickel to buy a paper. Then Jesse would return with the paper, sometimes also holding a chocolate bar in his mouth. Uncle Paddy was very lonely after Jesse was killed by a car as he crossed 3rd Avenue—hence the appointment at the taxidermist.

The only new picture hung in the saloon after Uncle Paddy's death was an elegant one of President John Fitzgerald Kennedy placed over the bar. The Irish, according to the writer Oscar Wilde, were the greatest talkers since the Greeks and, like the Greeks, they were interested in politics. Jacob Riis, the early 20th-century New York reformer, once remarked that "the Irishman's genius runs to public affairs rather than domestic life; wherever he is mustered in force, the saloon is the gorgeous center of political activity." I can only imagine the kind of political conversations that occurred at Clarke's bar in the early days when the Clarke brothers' lifelong interest in politics surely began.

I had been dating John Molanphy for about six months when John F. Kennedy's campaign for the presidency in 1960 put me in the middle of tension—loyalty to my father or to my new boyfriend. John's deceased father had often criticized Tammany Hall Democrats and, influenced by his father, John convinced me to vote for Richard Nixon over Kennedy. At the time I was fairly apolitical, even though I was a history major at Marymount College.

One evening after dinner, my dad said: "You are only voting against Kennedy because of that boy." He was absolutely right. And, unlike my father, I did not feel an allegiance to vote for JFK because he was an Irish Catholic. While my dad and three of his brothers had voted for the Republican Dwight D. Eisenhower in 1952 and 1956, the Democratic Kennedy was their choice in 1960. The other two brothers, Tom and Jim, both Catholic priests, were diehard Democrats all their lives. I have a strong memory of a friendly, but fierce, argument among the brothers in the basement party room of my Uncle Joe's house in Bayside, Long Island, over the 1952 election of Dwight Eisenhower over Adlai Stevenson. But I remember even more clearly the night my father became angry about my plan to vote for Richard Nixon.

While my then-boyfriend John and I had not voted for Kennedy in 1960, we both came to like him. Who could not have enjoyed the charm of the man? However, we also learned more about the president when John had a conversation with a special-service NYPD officer at Clarke's who said that President Kennedy was hard to guard because he had girlfriends in various places. We knew about Kennedy's indiscretions long before the rest of the country because the American press looked the other way about presidential scandals in those days. But while Kennedy was clearly a womanizer, he appeared

A portrait of the Irish Catholic President Kennedy hung over the bar.
Along with Marilyn Monroe, both Robert and Ted Kennedy frequented
P. J. Clarke's.

to have a great sense of humanity. His foreign policy—avoiding a world disaster during the Cuban missile crisis and his reevaluation of America's foreign policy on Vietnam—would influence our politics in later years.

In 1962 President Kennedy, who was fond of good food and liquor, signed a bill legalizing the serving of liquor at stand-up bars in Washington D.C.; Southern propriety had previously forbidden this type of drinking. Soon thereafter, an upscale saloon came to town—Clyde's opened in 1963 on M Street in Georgetown and was said to be inspired by P. J. Clarke's in Manhattan.

John and I read about Kennedy's trip to Ireland in the fall of 1962; JFK said that it was one of the most moving experiences of his life, and he promised to return again to the place he held with greatest of affections. He never did. John was on duty at P. J. Clarke's on November 22, 1963, when JFK was shot in Dallas, Texas. No one in the back room believed the terrible news when bartender Mike Murphy shouted out: "Kennedy's been shot in Dallas!" The men told Mike to stop joking around. Then the television made clear what had happened. Everybody crowded around the front bar to see the television coverage—people started crying, others left to go home—it was a very emotional afternoon.

Journalist Dorothy Kilgallen was still a frequenter of P. J. Clarke's, and she took a great interest in the assassination of President Kennedy. When she interviewed Jack Ruby, the killer of the accused assassin Lee Harvey Oswald, she told several associates that she planned to publish what she had learned from Ruby. But Kilgallen was never to reveal her findings from the interview—she was found dead from an overdose of alcohol and sleeping pills. Her death was ruled a suicide.

There is another theory about the cause of Kilgallen's death. Some believe she may have been murdered because of the information she might have revealed about the assassination of the president. Kilgallen was not known to be a "lush," nor did she use drugs, so the suicide theory seems weak.

A few years later, P. J. Clarke's would serve as the location for a conversation between historian Arthur Schlesinger, Jr. and Robert Kennedy, who both enjoyed the ambiance of the place. The two men discussed JFK's assassination on October 30, 1966, and Bobby admitted that he was not satisfied with the Warren Commission Report. Two years later, Bobby would be assassinated. In 1980 his only living brother, Ted, would visit P. J. Clarke's immediately after conceding defeat to President Jimmy Carter in the Democratic presidential primary election. The Kennedys liked Clarke's bar.

John Molanphy and I were married in August 1963, a few months before JFK's assassination. After the church ceremony that my Uncle Tom Clarke officiated, we partied with our guests at the Waldorf-Astoria Hotel, the place where we had first danced during our Emerald Ball blind date three years before.

Helen Marie with husband John on right – Joe Clarke, Helen, and
John Clarke on left – Helen is expecting her first son, Paul, in 1966

Mr. and Mrs. Daniel Lavezzo, Sr., the gracious and elegant owners of P. J. Clarke's, gave us a wedding gift—three handmade, black-and-gold frames to hold lithograph landscapes that came from my maternal great-grandfather Jimmy Dalton's homes on Sutton Place. John continued to work at P. J. Clarke's until he took a job at an advertising agency in 1965, but our favorite restaurant continued to be at 55th Street and 3rd Avenue.

CHAPTER NINE

Return to Clarke's Bar

ONE HOT SUMMER NIGHT IN 1975, JACK STERLING, NIGHT MANAGER at Clarke's, was seated at his usual small table in the corner of the front room, with his eye on the customers. Suddenly he got up and hobbled with his cane over to a young couple standing at the bar and snatched away their gin and tonics. Then Sterling wagged his finger in the girl's face and said, "I am going to tell your mother — you're under age — now go home." Sterling raised his cane at her for emphasis. She was seventeen-year-old Caroline Kennedy. My husband John, working once again at Clarke's, said that Caroline and her date left quickly.

From 1970 to 1975, John and I and our three sons, Paul, Brian, and Tom, lived in Pittsburgh, Pennsylvania, because John had taken a position in the media department at Ketchum, McLeod, and Grove Advertising. Little did we know that, like my grandaunt Alice McMahon, who returned from New York City to County Clare in the early 1900s, we would have our own "repatriation" story, leaving Pittsburgh to return to New York in 1975.

If you have ever watched the television program *Mad Men*, you know the advertising industry is volatile. When the job in Pittsburgh at Ketchum, McLeod, and Grove ended, we hiked back home to New York City with our three sons, ages four, five, and eight, unknowingly into the middle of the city's huge financial crisis. Our idea was that I would return to teaching social science in the New York City public high schools, while John looked for a new profession away from the uncertain field of advertising.

Instead, due to the extremely depressed New York City economy, John could not make a career change, and he took his old job back at P. J. Clarke's, assisting my Uncle Charlie with various duties, including tracking down customers who had passed bad checks. When John worked evenings, he was under the supervision of night manager Jack Sterling, a former society playboy, horse trainer, and night-club manager. Sterling had various ups and downs during his life, and he was hired by Dan Lavezzo, Jr. because he had experience at other restaurants around Manhattan.

Back at P. J. Clarke's, John relished other stories about the Kennedy family. Jackie Kennedy, always wearing her dark glasses, was a frequent visitor to the bar because she lived and worked in

Helen Marie in Kerry, Ireland, 1970 – she is expecting her
third son, Tom.

Manhattan as an editor at Alfred Knopf Publishing and later Viking Publishing. John said that the waiters were incredibly protective of Jackie's privacy, making sure that no one ever disturbed her, despite her notoriety. Her favorite meal was a hamburger and a spinach salad. Jackie was not new to 55th Street, nor was her second husband, Greek millionaire Aristotle Onassis, who had often accompanied Jackie's sister, Lee Radziwill, to Clarke's before his marriage to Jackie. It is said that Onassis proposed to Jackie at P. J. Clarke's. When they came for lunch, the couple enjoyed sitting at their window table, watching, while being watched.

John said that Jackie, now a widow for the second time, was often accompanied by well-known publishing personnel and authors for working lunches. On some Saturdays, Jackie brought John-John and Caroline for a meal. There was even an occasion when Jackie arrived on the arm of Frank Sinatra. John also heard that on another evening in the past Jackie had been accompanied by her brother-in-law, Bobby Kennedy. As she passed by the bouncer, Mark Tendler, she asked him if she could feel the muscles in his upper arm, and he agreed. Uncle Paddy must have been chuckling from his heavenly vantage point—the former First Lady in his bar.

Many of John's bartender and waiter friends from the 1960s were still working at Clarke's, and there were some new additions such as the Chinese American cleaning crew who were overseen by

A coaster from the 1204 N. State Parkway Chicago location of P. J. Clarke's, which licensed its name from the original.

a man whom staff called the "Mandarin" because he would just sit with his arms crossed, supervising his fellow immigrants.

Being ten years older now and with an increased interest in history, John took more note of the artifacts at P. J. Clarke's. He described the Tiffany-style glass window over the men's room and the ancient advertisement for Glenlivet whiskey. John chuckled over the "antique" mechanical cash registers, still used in the age of IBM. He also noted a new addition near the bar: a sign saying "UNITED NATIONS — WE BELIEVE."

Because I was becoming very interested in Irish history, John described all the portraits of Irish heroes hung at P. J. Clarke's: Robert Emmet, an 18th-century Irish aristocrat and rebel; Daniel O'Connell, known as the "Liberator" for his emancipation of Catholics in the early 19th century; Terence MacSwiney, mayor of Cork, who died on a politically based hunger strike in 1920; and Michael Collins, looking grim in his military uniform as he stood outside Dublin's General Post Office during the 1923 Civil War.

Dan Lavezzo, Jr. was now the owner of P. J. Clarke's because his parents were deceased. As a result, Dan Jr. made the bar his second home, being especially interested in the selection of the menu items and the music on the jukebox. Unlike the reputation of his more conservative parents, there were always stories circulating about Dan Jr.'s wins and losses at the racetrack. He had become an authority on thoroughbred breeding lineages and owned a Triple

The wine and beer list over a well-stocked bar – 2012

Crown candidate, named Charles Conerly for his good friend, the Giant football team's quarterback. Upstairs in the antique furnishings showroom above the bar, Dan Jr. created a library of books on thoroughbred horses.

His brother, John Lavezzo, a lover of Mountain Valley Water, preferred to play the trotters, including his own horse, at Roosevelt Field. The growth in popularity of the bar provided the brothers with the resources that allowed them to pursue their racing interests. An intelligent man, Dan Jr. also liked to discuss Freud and why people engaged in self-destructive behavior.

Dan Jr. was especially proud that Sinatra still said that P. J. Clarke's was the best place to end an evening and that "Ol' Blue Eyes" continued to be seen at table 20 with members of the Rat Pack. Like Lavezzo, Sinatra was the son of Italian immigrants. And, like the Irish, Frank was interested in politics, supporting JFK's election with large contributions (but later in life turning to finance Republicans Richard Nixon and Ronald Reagan).

Sinatra would favor P. J. Clarke's into his old age. He loved New York as well, as evidenced by his hit song, "New York, New York," which was first presented at Radio City Music Hall in 1978. There were many other occasions when Sinatra was involved in projects in New York City during the 1970s, so it was natural that he would end his evenings at one of his favorite spots, P. J. Clarke's. In 1973 he performed during a television special and issued an album entitled *Ol Blue Eyes Is Back*. The next year he starred in a televised concert at Madison Square Garden. Leroy Neiman's 1978 painting, "P. J. Clarke's - An Irish-American Saloon," features Frank Sinatra in the first row by the bar, near the table where Jacqueline Kennedy is also portrayed.

Frank Sinatra was always hounded by the FBI, who suspected that he had Mafia associations, especially in Las Vegas, Nevada. Dan Lavezzo Jr. did not have a mob reputation, but diners could occasionally catch a glimpse of gangster Frank Costello meandering through the entrance on 55th Street. In fact, one evening the waiters were faced with a unique triangle of celebrities—Mafia boss "the Prime Minister" Frank Costello, former Vice President Hubert Humphrey, and Marilyn Monroe sitting at individual tables waiting for their guests. The rest of the room was empty.

Politicians like Humphrey were flocking to P. J. Clarke's. New York Governor Hugh Carey was a regular and was eventually asked to pay his bill, though publicly he denied that he came to the saloon that often. Harlem Congressman Reverend Adam Clayton Powell Jr. would enter the front entrance on 3rd Avenue with a blonde on one arm and a redhead on the other and would proudly stroll the length of the bar, showing off his women. Occasionally there were also famous political visitors such as Ted Kennedy and Ronald Reagan.

On any given night, customers might see actresses Hedy Lamarr, Alice Faye, Geraldine Page, or Liza Minnelli. My husband said that Liza was "pixie, pert, and pretty," with a lively, vivacious personality. Liza wore classic little black dresses in a soft velvet material, with very simple sterling ball earrings, silver necklaces, and bracelets. Her black suede, high-heeled, open-toed shoes were decorated with silver buckles. Liza often arrived with her agent, and they chatted amicably throughout their meal. As usual, the staff made sure that she was not bothered by any autograph seekers. To this day, Liza is a faithful and enthusiastic customer.

Liz Smith, the New York society journalist, was a regular who would order a beer on draft with a burger and fries. She liked to praise Dan Lavezzo, Jr. as "Mr. New York." One night Johnny Mercer sat at the bar while his favorite bartender, Tommy Joyce, was serving him. After several hours, Mercer composed the words to his song "One for My Baby, (and One More for the Road)" on a napkin. He turned to Joyce and apologized to him for not using Tommy's name in the song—he could not make it work, and instead he wrote "Set Em Up, Joe," for the song that Frank Sinatra would make famous. Tommy Joyce would continue to be sought after as a "father confessor" by many steady customers like Mercer.

Adding to the "mythical" nature of P. J. Clarke's, singer Nat King Cole pronounced Clarke's bacon cheeseburger as the "Cadillac of burgers," and the *New York Times* declared that P. J. Clarke's was the "Vatican of saloons." Actor and known alcoholic Richard Harris agreed with Nat King Cole, saying that he adored

P. J. Clarke's cheeseburger. Harris always bragged about arriving at P. J. Clarke's and getting an automatic setup of six double vodkas from the bartender. Another actor, Christopher Plummer, was involved in a startling scene at the bar. One night he rode his motorcycle into the side door of P. J. Clarke's with actor Jason Robards on the back. The cycle had hit the curb and crashed into the door, winding up at their reserved table. Plummer says their order of Jack Daniels followed, the bartenders thinking nothing of their arrival.

Though the menu was supervised by Dan Jr., Charlie Clarke was the man who ran the liquor department. During the 1970s, the most popular drink at P. J. Clarke's was a Bloody Mary. Martinis with olives or Gibsons with onions were the most sought after gin and vodka drinks. Other popular mixed drinks were Manhattans, Rob Roys, and grasshoppers. Beer was served on draft and if you ordered a beer without specifying which kind, you got Michelob. Heineken's, Wurzburger, Dortmunder, and Watney's Red Barrel Ale were also served on tap. In addition, a vast array of imported bottled beers was available. The tap room was right under the bar, a refrigerated locker from which heavy rubber lines ran from the kegs up through the floor to the spigots on the bar. In Uncle Paddy's day 200 pound blocks of ice had been the refrigeration method, and the Lavezzo family continued this tradition into the 1980s, allowing the "iceman to cometh" to Clarke's.

Large blocks of ice had always been used at the saloon for another reason. A feature at P. J. Clarke's was the men's room with its stained glass dome over the entry and very large shoulder-height, semicircular, 100-year-old urinals made of white porcelain. The men's huge urinals were once described by Frank Sinatra in an interview: "You could stand (Mayor) Abe Beame in one of them and have room to spare." From Uncle Paddy's era up until the 1970s, blocks of ice were placed in the urinals several times a day—an original form of deodorizer. This practice was stopped when the Lavezzos got tired of the flooding that resulted.

The ladies' room was extremely small, perhaps because women were a minority of the population at the saloon. One day when John was on duty, a young woman walked into the bar and tried to apply for a job. As she made her inquiry, one of Dan Jr.'s friends, who hung out daily at P. J. Clarke's, told her, "We don't hire women here." That young lady was determined, and she filed a discrimination suit with a New York employment board. She was hired at the bar several weeks later.

As a girl, it never struck me as unfair that we always entered Clarke's bar through the "ladies' entrance," or that women were not allowed at the front bar. I accepted it as the way things were. But then the feminist movement began, and in the era of Germaine Greer, I bristled when in 1973 a magazine salesman invited my husband and me to a Pittsburgh club where women had

The elegant men's washroom sign – 2012

Photo © Greg Naeseth

to climb the back staircase to enter the dining room. The salesman got an earful when I joined the two men at the table.

So I was pleased to hear that the young woman had been hired at P. J. Clarke's.

During the two years from 1975 to 1977 when John worked at the saloon, I would bring our sons to see their dad and share a meal with him. We were enjoying being back in New York, close to our two families and to the culture of the city. However, it was not an easy choice we had made. There were lots of ups and downs for me in the financially handicapped New York City public schools. I was just hitting my stride teaching when I almost lost my job at a high school due to a clerical mistake in my records of employment at the New York City Board of Education. A clerk had eliminated two years of my service, and this made me liable to be transferred from my high school to a school even further away from my home.

While I was able to get the error corrected, the stress and the fact that John and I were finding it difficult to be together as a family due to our hours had us concerned. So, when a call came from John's friend, Larry, head of media at Tracy Locke Advertising in Dallas, Texas, John accepted the job. In 1977 we moved to Texas, where we would live for the next twenty-two years, many miles from P. J. Clarke's.

CHAPTER TEN

The Little Bar That Still Could

ON ONE OF JOHN'S LAST DAYS AT P. J. CLARKE'S, HE WAS introduced to a couple from Dallas, Texas, who had attended the Democratic presidential convention in Manhattan and were celebrating Jimmy Carter's nomination. Joe was a realtor and would sell us our home on Norway Road in Dallas, and his journalist wife Ann would provide me with a copy of a *Dallas Times Herald* investigation of the Texas prison system in the 1950s that became central to my doctoral dissertation at the University of Texas. This is an example of the "magic" of P. J. Clarke's, where many connections and arrangements have been made, a reflection of the Irish networking system. In my case, the tie to Ann and her journalism report had a profound influence, as it led to my spending two years of my life researching and visiting the Texas prisons. To this

The little bar that could – 2012

Photo © Greg Naeseth

day, some of the college-level courses I teach concern the American criminal justice system.

Recently, while doing research on police corruption, I came upon an interesting scenario. Bill Philipps, a regular customer at P. J. Clarke's, but a corrupt NYPD narcotics detective, agreed to be an informant for a police investigative body during a meeting at the saloon. When he began to play both sides, he was picked up at P. J. Clarke's and brought down to police headquarters, and later imprisoned. Uncle Paddy would have enjoyed the story.

Our visits to P. J. Clarke's would be greatly reduced in the years we lived in Texas, but my attachment to the place seemed to grow—perhaps the saloon came to represent "home" for me, as my mother and father had died in the 1980s and my siblings were living elsewhere. My immediate family was gone, but the place where my father and his five brothers had lived was still in existence. As a newcomer in Texas, I also began to appreciate how hard migration must have been for Uncle Paddy when he crossed the Atlantic.

Family members continued to pass on stories of P. J. Clarke's in the 1980s and 1990s to their Texas relative. Celebrities still frequented the saloon, including new additions such as singers Johnny Mathis and Sarah Vaughan. Latin American novelist Mario Vargas Llosa liked the bar and, in later years, would comment on how much he always enjoyed a meal of eggs Benedict and a Bloody Mary at P. J. Clarke's. A high school friend wrote to me about enjoying the sight of Woody Allen keeping time to the music played by a group of jazz musicians who regularly took a table in the back room of Clarke's. If you were lucky, you might see Woody joining them on his clarinet. Being a reclusive sort, Woody really appreciated the fact that P. J.'s respected his sense of privacy and did not publicize his presence at the bar.

When Claus von Bulow was on trial in New York for causing the death of his socialite wife, he regularly appeared for a meal at P. J. Clarke's. One sarcastic pundit claimed that von Bulow was getting ready for prison food, though customers still found the menu at Clarke's to be good.

Von Bulow was eventually found not guilty after an appeals process that only a wealthy man could afford. There were days when von Bulow could not use the phone booth at P. J. Clarke's because a local bookmaker occupied it for hours, an aberration, despite the police presence. Criminal types were not welcome, but in the 1990s John Gotti, the notorious Mafia figure, began eating dinner at P. J. Clarke's—Dan Jr.'s son, Dan III, was not pleased and said it would not be good for the saloon, despite the fact that Gotti paid cash and left a $25 tip.

P. J. Clarke's had been grossing good amounts of money, and Dan Jr. had opened an additional restaurant in the basement of

Modern-day oyster bar at P. J. Clarke's

Macy's department store on 34th Street, where Mary Tyler Moore, Keith Richards, and John Lithgow became regulars. The Macy's location lasted through the 1980s. After Dan Jr. closed that restaurant, he tried to found another P. J. Clarke's in a new location, but he couldn't find investors.

Charles Clarke, one of the four brothers born over the saloon, retired from his position as manager in 1989, and Dan Jr. attended his going-away party at Kennedy's bar on East 57th Street. Tired of his own role as owner, Dan Jr. passed the baton to Dan III. Eleven years later, in 2000, Dan Lavezzo, Jr. died of heart failure at age eighty-three, just before a third set of owners would take on the job of running the saloon.

In the summer of 2000, I flew into Manhattan to attend the fiftieth anniversary of my Uncle Tom Clarke becoming a Jesuit priest. Looking as young and fit as ever, Uncle Tom met me at my hotel on East 57th Street and treated me to a visit at the Museum of Natural History, where we sat in comfortable, reclining chairs in the planetarium and listened to the recorded voice of Tom Hanks tell us about the universe.

After our visit to the Museum of Natural History, Uncle Tom and I made our way over to the Metropolitan Museum. Then, finally, we walked to P. J. Clarke's for dinner. The Irish American waiters greeted us warmly; after all, we were Charlie Clarke's family. P. J. Clarke's showed no sign of change, even though New York

City continued to evolve—new buildings arising all the time among the many landmarks.

Uncle Tom began reminiscing about his home upstairs over the bar. Here was this eminent theologian showing nostalgia for a flat over what had been a speakeasy. It was the only home Uncle Tom had known outside of the seminaries and retreat centers in which he had lived as a Jesuit priest. In contrast to this ascetic, male-only environment, Uncle Tom had grown up over a pleasure-seeking bar located near a noisy train. Only the male atmosphere was the same.

Sitting there with Tom, I reaffirmed my old intention to write about this saloon, and it was my uncle who suggested the title *Over P. J.'s*. The two of us ended the evening by sharing a piece of New York–style cheesecake and taking a long walk around town. I could hardly keep up with the man who, at seventeen, had lost one lung due to tuberculosis. The summer of 2000 was the last time I saw my Uncle Tom, such a good friend. He passed away in 2005.

Four years later, Uncle Charlie, manager of P. J. Clarke's and the man who made the saloon work, joined Uncle Tom in exiting this world. He had seen a great deal during his forty-three years "behind the stick," pulling down the beer handle at the mahogany bar. When asked by one of his sons about the changes he had witnessed, Uncle Charlie's response was, "We used to have to speak to a fellow occasionally for using bad language in front of women, but now the women use bad language in front of the men. And it

Brian Molanphy, Helen Marie's middle son, with Charlie Clarke,
manager of P. J. Clarke's - Chalkboard Menu – 1988

was easier to cut off a drunk years ago. You could just say, 'Go,' and he'd leave out of respect. Today, you have to read them their rights." As Uncle Charlie could attest, even when surrounded by famous people, being a saloon keeper is not as glamorous as some might think.

When Dan III took over the ownership of the saloon, he had made a few minor changes, such as turning the old jukebox with its records into a CD jukebox. Always the domain of his father, the songs played were eclectic, including tunes by Louis Armstrong, Frank Sinatra, Tony Bennett, Alice Faye, Patsy Cline, Lotte Lenya, Edith Piaf, Judy Holliday, Chet Baker, and Hoagy Carmichael, most of whom were customers. Dan III added Brazilian music because his mother was from Brazil, and he had lived there with her after his parents' divorce.

A serious young man, Dan III still faced financial difficulties. In 1999 the new owners of the building, Reckson Association Realty Corporation, brought suit, stating that Dan III was behind on rent and utility bills; in March 2001 a civil court ruled that the Lavezzo family lease had come to an end. Dan III filed for bankruptcy, but once again the "little bar that could" was not shut down because the Reckson Corporation saw the benefit of the saloon to their holdings. Before he died, Dan Lavezzo, Jr. had made the comment that he wanted continuity and a similar style for the saloon no matter who owned it. His wish has been fulfilled.

Led by Phil Scotti, a prominent New York restaurant owner and long-time fan of Clarke's, the Reckson Corporation found twenty investors to take over the saloon, including real estate giants Stephen Siegel and Arnold Penner, baseball magnate George Steinbrenner, and actor Timothy Hutton. Scotti, a faithful Clarke's customer for many years, is the owner of two New York enterprises, Sarabeth's and Docks Oyster Bar, as well as other restaurants. He brought the necessary experience to the endeavor and, ironically, has a surname that once described the tribe from Ireland who settled Scotland, the Scotti.

The enterprise, called Clarke's Group, is leasing the saloon for twenty years. From his heavenly vantage point, Uncle Paddy must be intrigued. If he had not agreed to Billy Wilder's filming the saloon for *The Lost Weekend*, P. J. Clarke's might not be famous today. Deceased Dan Lavezzo, Jr. must be proud as well, because his family saved the property from being condemned in the 1960s. And all the years of manager Charlie Clarke's conscientious work provided a great foundation.

However, the physical foundation of the saloon was questionable. Finding structural flaws in the building, Phil Scotti announced that he would renovate the bar and would double its capacity by adding a second-floor restaurant called Sidecar. Scotti said that he simply wanted P. J. Clarke's to be alive again. He has done more than that by opening two other P. J. Clarke's bars in

Joe, Tom, Charlie, and Ray Clarke – New York, 2001

Manhattan—one at Lincoln Center and the other at the World Financial Center downtown. Scotti duplicated the saloon on K Street in Washington D.C. and again in Las Vegas, Nevada, where the P. J. Clarke's is 12,000 square feet in size and seats 323 people in the dining rooms and bars. Clarke's Group also went international by opening a branch in Sao Paulo, Brazil. All of these P. J. Clarke locations are up and running and successful.

When Clarke's Group began its renovation plans for the original saloon on 55th Street and 3rd Avenue, newspapers estimated the expense at between $0.5 million and $3 million, but the redo eventually cost more than $4 million. The saloon was gutted, and memorabilia were stored in a Long Island City warehouse after being laser measured and documented on film. Structural steel beams replaced the old wooden ones that were failing. The small kitchen that served burgers by the bar was now serving oysters.

A big investment for the Clarke's Group was the creation of the Sidecar restaurant on the second floor, encompassing the area where Paddy Clarke and my father's family lived for so many years. Sidecar has a sophisticated menu and features a speakeasy theme— a separate entrance with an intercom and a key card for members. If you are lucky, Phil Scotti's wife, Thea, a talented woman from England, will be on duty and welcome you to your table.

Downstairs, Clarke's Group kept the mahogany bar, Jesse, (the stuffed dog), and the large urinals, as well as an out-of-order pay phone and cigarette machine. One pundit has written that these two machines never worked because Paddy Clarke did not like technology; however, my husband recalls that during both of his working periods at the saloon, the pay phone and the cigarette machine worked, as did the jukebox. The latter, playing Frank Sinatra and Tony Bennett tunes, can now be heard all over the restaurant and bar.

The new owners did not replace the mirrors streaked with age, nor did they remove customer Phil Kennedy's ashes from their resting place. That gentleman had been a baseball infielder with the Cardinals and frequented P. J. Clarke's. Kennedy would sit all day on a Sunday watching the Giants play, and during the week he would get his telephone messages at the bar. He was a fixture and left instructions for his daughter to have his ashes placed at P. J. Clarke's, which she did. His ashes have as their companion a portrait of deceased baseball owner, George Steinbrenner.

On reopening day, an elderly woman who lived in the neighborhood entered the 3rd Avenue doors of P. J. Clarke's, took a good look around, and said, "What were you doing in here all year? It looks exactly the same." Phil Scotti took that as a compliment, but he did make some changes to the blackboard menu, claiming that the staff had found recipes dating back to 1932. Additions included leek and potato soup, shepherd's pie, and chicken pot pie. Some customers have criticized the new burgers as being too bland, and not the same old juicy, fatty ones that Nat King Cole praised as the "Cadillac of burgers." There is serious talk of owner Scotti creating a hamburger stand somewhere in Manhattan, and perhaps the old recipe will be found. Meanwhile, Scotti is using fine, grass-fed beef from Montana, and his sixty-five-acre farm in upstate New York provides the fresh produce.

As for the bar itself, Phil Scotti is quoted as saying, "Our old-school bartenders serve up bourbon the right way—no ice." He made a good selection in his bartender, Doug Quinn, who was profiled in an article by Frank Bruni of the *New York Times* under the heading "The Bartender of Your Dreams." On my visit to P. J. Clarke's in October 2011, the gracious manager, Brian Carter, introduced me to Quinn, who took a moment from his busy schedule to say hello. Quinn is known to be a magician behind the mahogany bar—filling beer glasses without looking at them and having a reputation for making great cocktails and never forgetting who ordered what.

Phil Scotti is eager to keep the atmosphere of the saloon alive— he understands the charisma of the place. In my October 2011 conversation with Scotti, he emphasized how much he wants people to enjoy the ambiance, the excellent service, and the good food and drink. Scotti repeated something he had said before: "When you walk into our joint we automatically assume you are an old friend." While Scotti stated that he sees P. J. Clarke's as a welcoming place for "everyman," it is clear that the saloon continues to attract many celebrities.

When asked, customers say that they still favor the original saloon on 55th Street because the ghosts are felt in its walls. One reviewer on Citysearch.com wrote, "It [Clarke's] had the personality of a restaurant that felt the pulse of a city and made people feel they were part of history." And I am also most comfortable in the old place that is now officially an Upper East Side historical landmark. Of course, the expansion to so many locations is also a tribute to my Uncle Paddy's hard work, a fulfillment of his dreams as a young man stepping off the ship that brought him to New York, and a salute to his memory.

The bar that witnessed Brendan Behan typing his stories is the same one in which writer Eugene O'Neill once stood drinking his whiskey. P. J. Clarke's continues to draw ordinary folks and famous people through its doors on 3rd Avenue. Some say that the ghost of Paddy Clarke may wander the saloon. I was recently able to send Clarke's Group a framed picture of Uncle Paddy, so he now has a visible presence in his old hangout. If we could hear him, he might offer this Irish blessing: "As you slide down the banister of life, may the splinters not be pointing the wrong way."

And may his saloon last another 100 years.

Nick Molanphy, Helen Marie's grandson, age 10, New York – 2006

Author Biography

HELEN MARIE CLARKE IS A GRANDNIECE OF PATRICK JOSEPH CLARKE, founder of the legendary P. J. Clarke's Bar in New York City. Her father and his five brothers were brought up in a tenement flat on the second floor Over P. J.'s, and Clarke's bar forms an intrinsic part of her family history.

Helen Marie, a mother and a grandmother, lives in Santa Fe, New Mexico, with her husband John Molanphy. She has her doctorate in humanities from the University of Texas and teaches in the liberal arts departments of Santa Fe Community College and Santa Fe University of Art and Design. Helen Marie has written a second memoir, *Through the Ladies' Entrance: Tales from Schools,*

Sanctuaries and the Auld Sod. She is completing a historical novel, *Leaving Lissadell,* which is a rendering of the life of Irish heroine Constance Gore-Booth Markiewicz. Helen Marie enjoys offering a workshop entitled "Healing through Writing" at various locations in the Southwest.

A New York History Viewing List

1920s: *Great Gatsby, Jazz Singer*

1930s: *Once Upon a Time in America, Untouchables, Some Like it Hot, Radio Days*

1940s: *Easter Parade, New York, New York, An Affair to Remember, Lost Weekend*

1950s: *How to Marry a Millionaire, Sabrina, Guys and Dolls*

1960s: *Breakfast at Tiffany's, Barefoot in the Park*

1970s: *Annie Hall* (and all other Woody Allen films)

1980s: *Wall Street, Moonstruck*

The front door reflecting the bustling Manhattan neighborhood that P. J. Clarke's has called home for over 100 years.